THE BULFINCH ANATOMY OF
ANTIQUE
FURNITURE

THE BULFINCH ANATOMY OF
ANTIQUE
FURNITURE

AN ILLUSTRATED GUIDE TO
IDENTIFYING PERIOD, DETAIL, AND DESIGN

TIM FORREST
CONSULTING EDITOR PAUL ATTERBURY

BULFINCH PRESS
NEW YORK • BOSTON

Bulfinch Press

Time Warner Book Group
1271 Avenue of the Americas
New York, NY 10020
Visit our Web site at www.bulfinchpress.com

First North American Edition
Fourth Printing, 2004

ISBN 0-8212-2325-9

Library of Congress Catalog Card Number
96-76459

PROJECT EDITOR Anne Yelland
DESIGN The Design Revolution
PICTURE EDITOR Elizabeth Loving

Conceived, edited, and designed by
MARSHALL EDITIONS
The Old Brewery,
6 Blundell Street,
London N7 9BH

Origination by HBM Print, Singapore
Printed and bound in China
by Midas Printing International Limited

CONTENTS

INTRODUCTION

Whether you are a potential buyer of antiques or an appreciative appraiser of family heirlooms, this book is intended to make you really look at antique furniture. It is vital, of course, if you are thinking of buying any antique piece that it appeals to you, and that it is something you want to have it in your home.

But equally important is knowing what you are buying: whether it is completely period (that is, made when its style was first popular); whether it has been altered or restored; or whether it is a later copy, since many styles have enjoyed revivals in popularity. This may sound daunting, but above all, this book will make you better informed about how pieces are put together; what to the uninformed may look right, but is wrong; what is good or bad; what is pure and what adulterated.

Furniture has a long history, so here the field is narrowed to include pieces from the 17th to the early 20th centuries – the period from which most of the antique furniture found today derives. The book covers the major types of furniture, from different periods and of different designs. Since it is such an important area that

continues to grow in popularity among collectors, country furniture is covered separately. Small occasional pieces, mirrors, painted and lacquered furniture, as well as outdoor and sunroom furniture, are also included.

The featured pieces range from the relatively common to the rare, but all have been chosen to explain and illustrate how the age and style of an item can be judged. Constructional and decorative details are highlighted, as are the woods from which pieces are made. This is useful both as a guide to dating and as an indicator of where a piece was made. The examples are drawn from many sources both to pinpoint national stylistic idiosyncracies and to demonstrate the way in which certain styles transcend national frontiers.

Furniture plays an important role in our everyday lives, from the desks and chairs we use at work to the comfortable beds to which we retire. But antique furniture is more than merely functional: it is esthetically pleasing and offers a real link with the past. An in-depth knowledge of such pieces can only enhance appreciation of them, and this book provides that knowledge.

ITALIAN CASSONE
The often elaborate carving or other decoration on Italian cassoni bely their usually simple construction. They are essentially boxes, joined by mortise and tenon joints, and with a hinged lid.

CHIPPENDALE SOFA FRAME
Nowhere is the anatomy of furniture more apparent than when the upholstery and trimmings are removed from a chair or sofa. This frame shows the basic structure of the sofa; how the visible parts of the frame might be carved or decorated, while those that would not be seen were untreated; and the nail holes of repeated coverings.

HOW TO USE THIS BOOK

The information in this book is presented in three different ways. Each chapter begins with two or more annotated illustrations of archetypal pieces covered in detail in the chapter, so that all the technical terms that occur in the chapter are clear, and major features of specific relevance to that chapter are highlighted. This is followed by a digest of stylistic or constructional features and variations, to provide an at-a-glance reference – by date – of common, interesting, or unusual design details.

The rest of the book is dedicated to two-page treatments of pieces of furniture. There is one main image of a piece that is typical of the style or period under discussion, or of interest because of its history or esthetic appeal, or because it was made by a renowned cabinetmaker. This piece is analysed in detail, and features of special interest are pinpointed in words and secondary images. Alongside it are complementary pieces which either demonstrate the development of a style or offer alternative interpretations of it.

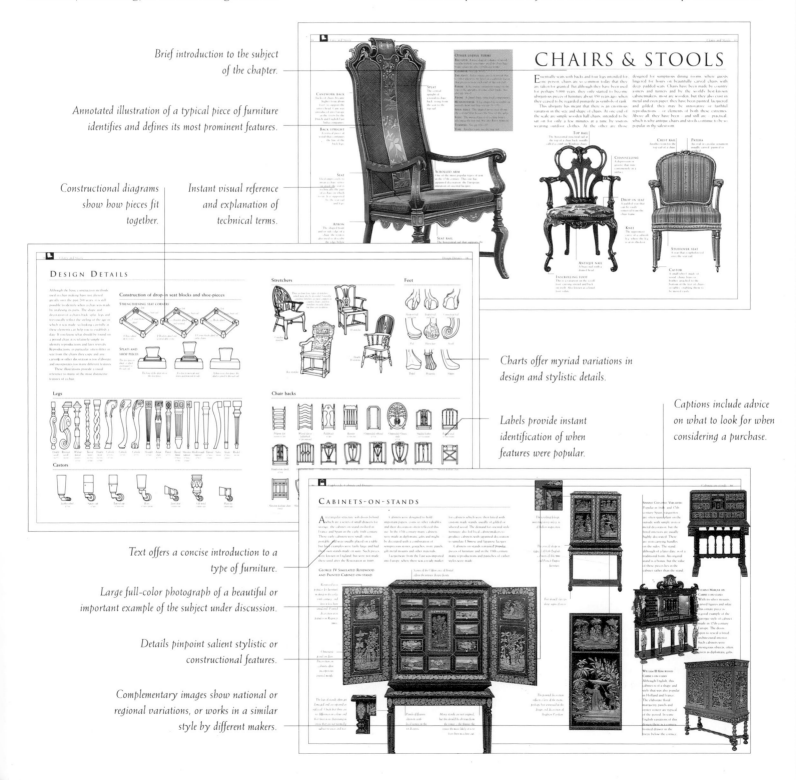

Brief introduction to the subject of the chapter.

Annotated illustration of a typical piece of furniture identifies and defines its most prominent features.

Constructional diagrams show how pieces fit together.

Instant visual reference and explanation of technical terms.

Charts offer myriad variations in design and stylistic details.

Labels provide instant identification of when features were popular.

Captions include advice on what to look for when considering a purchase.

Text offers a concise introduction to a type of furniture.

Large full-color photograph of a beautiful or important example of the subject under discussion.

Details pinpoint salient stylistic or constructional features.

Complementary images show national or regional variations, or works in a similar style by different makers.

USEFUL TERMS

Decorative techniques and ornaments

Anthemion

Berlin woolwork

Capital

Caryatid

Cup and cover

Escutcheon

ACANTHUS *Leaf pattern widely used in classical antiquity and revived during the Renaissance as an ornamental motif in carving and decoration.*

AMORINI *Carved figures of boys particularly used on furniture of the 17th-century and later.*

AMPHORA *Classical two-handled jar for transporting wine or oil, revived in the 18th century as a decorative motif in the repertoire of neoclassical design.*

ANTHEMION *Stylized flower motif based on honeysuckle and derived from a classical Greek ornament. Used in the 18th and 19th centuries on furniture, silverware, and in decoration.*

APPLIED DECORATION *An ornamental finish prepared in advance and glued, or glued and screwed to an object in a completed state.*

ARCADING *Decorative feature, found on furniture and carved panels of the late 16th and the 17th century, taking the form of a series of rounded arches.*

ASTRAGAL *Half-round molding attached to the edges of cupboards or door frames to conceal the joint; also used for glazing bars on glass-fronted cupboards.*

BALUSTER *Turned column with a curving shape, used on table legs, chair backs, glass stems, metalware, and ceramics.*

BANDING *Narrow decorative strips of veneer or inlay, usually forming a border. Straight banding is cut with the grain; crossbanding is cut across the grain; herringbone or feather banding is cut diagonally across the grain. See p. 66.*

BANTAMWORK *Incised lacquer decoration common on Dutch and English furniture, also known as cutwork.*

BARLEY-SUGAR TWIST *Type of turning in which the wood is shaped in a spiral; used on legs, columns, or for decoration. See pp. 126–27.*

BERLIN WOOLWORK *Wool needlework depicting pastoral or religious scenes, landscapes, or flowers, used on upholstery, screens, etc in the 19th century.*

BEVEL *The slanted edge of a pane of glass or mirror cut to form a decorative border.*

BOBBIN TURNING *A series of wooden spheres turned on a lathe, used on 17th- and 18th-century chair and table legs and stretchers. See pp. 126–27.*

BOSS *Oval or circular ornamental projection used to cover a joint in moldings.*

BOULLEWORK *Style of marquetry, also known as buhlwork, using tortoiseshell and brass inlay, perfected by Louis XIV's cabinetmaker, André-Charles Boulle, in the early 18th century.*

CABLE MOLDING *Closely twisted reeding resembling nautical rope used on Regency furniture.*

CABOCHON *Round or oval raised decoration, often used in conjunction with acanthus leaves or shellwork on cabriole legs, popular in the 18th century.*

CAPITAL *The head of a column or pilaster.*

CARTOUCHE *Decoratively shaped tablet, often enclosed by scrollwork and used to frame crests or coats-of-arms.*

CARYATID *Support in the form of the female figure, particularly popular on rococo and neoclassical pieces.*

CHEVRON *Any V-shaped pattern; popular on Gothic revival and Art Deco pieces.*

CHIP CARVING *Design made in a wooden panel by chipping out a pattern; found from the medieval period to the early 17th century.*

COCKBEADING *A beaded molding that projects from the surface of a piece of furniture; most common on drawer fronts.*

COQUILLAGE *Decoration incorporating a shell motif, used on rococo-style furniture.*

CRESTING *Carved decoration along the top rail of a chair, mirror frame, or cabinet.*

CROSSBANDING *Thin strips of cross-grained veneer.*

C SCROLL *Decorative device based on the letter C, popular on rococo furniture.*

CUP AND COVER *Bulbous, turned-wood decoration found on legs of furniture and on bedposts in Elizabethan and 19th-century revival styles.*

CURL VENEER *Veneer cut from the fork where a branch joins the trunk of a tree, valued for its decorative grain.*

DENTIL MOLDING *Series of equally spaced blocks said to resemble teeth, used on 18th-century and later furniture.*

EGG AND DART *Carved or molded ornamentation found on furniture, in particular cabinets, consisting of a series of ovals alternating with arrowheads.*

ENTABLATURE *Architectural term adopted by cabinetmakers for the components surmounting a column: the architrave, frieze, and cornice.*

ESCUTCHEON *Decorative metal plate surrounding a keyhole on furniture; also a carved shield on a pediment.*

FESTOON *Motif shaped like a garland of flowers or fruit or swag of drapery, popular on baroque and neoclassical furniture.*

FINIAL *Carved, turned, or metal ornament mounted on top of a piece of furniture, such as a bureau bookcase or chair back. See p. 107.*

FLUTING *Vertical cut or groove on a cylindrical object such as a column.*

FRENCH POLISH *Lacquered furniture finish introduced in the late 18th century.*

FRETWORK *Technique of cutting thin pieces of wood or metal into shapes or patterns with a fine-bladed saw.*

GADROONING *Carved or molded border consisting of a series of raised convex curves; also used on silver and ceramics.*

GESSO *A type of plaster made from powdered chalk and size which, when many layers are applied to wood or other materials, gives a hard, smooth base for painting or gilding and can be carved.*

GUILLOCHE *A pattern of intertwined ribbons, worked in single or double bands, resulting in a series of small circles.*

HERRINGBONE BANDING *Two narrow strips of veneer with grain running in opposite directions. See p. 66.*

INLAY *Technique whereby contrasting woods, metals such as brass, ivory, mother-of-pearl, and other materials are set into recesses cut into the surface of a piece.*

INTARSIA *Inlaid still life or architectural scene made of different colored woods, used on furniture in the 16th and 17th centuries.*

JAPANNING *Technique originating in the early 18th century whereby European craftsmen imitated oriental lacquerwork with paint and varnish.*

LACQUER *Several layers of a hard glossy resin, from the tree Rhus vernicifera, built up and carved or inlaid with various materials. True lacquer originates in the Orient and was mainly used there, but European craftsmen sought to imitate it in various ways.*

LAMBREQUIN *A piece of wood carved to simulate swags of drapery with elaborate, often gilded, tassels hanging down.*

LUNETTE *Decoration of repeated carved or pierced half moons.*

MARQUETRY *Floral, landscape, or other representational pattern of veneer in woods of contrasting grains and patterns. See p. 45.*

MOLDING *Raised strip of plaster or wood applied to a piece as decoration, often also used to conceal a joint.*

OGEE *Double curve, convex at the top and becoming concave at the bottom, often found on moldings and on the feet of Georgian furniture. See pp. 108–109.*

ORMOLU *The powdered gold used to gild furniture mounts made from bronze and other metals; now also the mounts themselves.*

OVOLO *Decorative molding of convex quarter-circle section.*

OYSTER VENEER *Type of veneer using sections cut across the grain from the branches of walnut or laburnum trees, whose pattern resembles an oyster. See p. 45.*

PALMETTE *Neoclassical fan-shaped motif.*

PAPIER-MÂCHÉ *A mix of paper pulp, water, sand, and chalk which can molded and shaped and hardens when dry. Used for furniture in the 19th century.*

PARCEL GILDING *Part gilding of a piece of furniture; ungilded areas are protected with varnish or shellac.*

PARQUETRY *Form of marquetry based on a repeated, geometric pattern, worked in contrasting woods. See p. 45.*

PATERA *Circular or oval motif decorated in low relief and widely used as an ornament on neoclassical furniture.*

PIE CRUST *Scalloped decorative rim fashionable in the 18th and 19th centuries.*

PIETRA DURA *Semiprecious stones and marble used as inlay on tables and cabinets.*

PUTTI *Decorative cupids or cherubs.*

REEDING *Decoration similar to fluting, but instead of carved grooves, convex parallel ribs are carved in the wood.*

ROCAILLE *Rococo decoration of abstract shell-like devices.*

ROUNDEL *Small ornamental medallion or disk, sometimes incorporating a head in profile.*

SPANDREL *A curved, triangular, or shaped bracket in an otherwise open corner.*

STRINGING *Inlay on furniture consisting of fine lines of metal or contrasting wood.*

TREFOIL *Gothic ornament consisting of three symmetrical leaf shapes, popular during the 19th-century Gothic revival.*

TURNING *Using a lathe to shape wood, metal, or other material. Also known as turnery. See pp. 126–27.*

VENEER *Thin sheet of attractively grained wood such as satinwood, rosewood, or walnut applied to a surface for decorative effect. Practiced since ancient times, veneering was fashionable in Europe from the 17th century.*

VERNIS MARTIN *Form of lacquer patented by Guillaume Martin and his brother in the 18th century.*

Cabinetmakers and designers

ADAM, ROBERT (1728–92) *Scottish architect and designer who, with his brother James, revived classical ornamentation and design in a style that bears their name.*

BELTER, JOHN HENRY (1804–63) *One of New York's foremost designers and a leading exponent of the rococo revival style. He created elaborate lacy pieces from laminated rosewood panels using a technique that he patented.*

BOULLE, ANDRÉ CHARLES (1642–1732) *Cabinetmaker to Louis XIV who is best known for boullework (see Decorative techniques).*

CHIPPENDALE, THOMAS (1718–79) *English cabinetmaker and designer. Most of the 160 designs in his book* The Gentleman and Cabinet-Maker's Director *first published in 1754, are in Chinese, Gothic, or French rococo style. Lacquering, painting, or gilding were used to finish many of the pieces.*

EASTLAKE, CHARLES LOCKE (1836–1906) *British architect and designer whose book* Hints on Household Taste *(1868) revived interest in the "Early English" style in the late 19th century.*

GILLOWS (WARING AND GILLOW) *English company during the 18th and 19th centuries producing well-designed high-quality machine-made furniture, some of it in the Gothic revival style initiated by Pugin.*

GODWIN, EDWARD (1833–86) *Disciple of the Aesthetic movement who incorporated elements of Japanese style into his designs.*

HEPPLEWHITE, GEORGE (d.1786) *English cabinetmaker and furniture designer, an exponent of the neoclassical style, best known for his* Cabinet-Maker and Upholsterer's Guide *published in 1788. It contained 300 designs characterized by simplicity, elegance, and utility.*

INCE AND MAYHEW *Partnership making gothic, chinoiserie and neoclassical furniture.*

JACOB, GEORGES (1739–1814) *Leading French menuisier of the pre-Revolutionary period, who worked in the neoclassical style.*

KENT, WILLIAM (1684–1748) *Architect and designer in the classical style.*

LANNUIER, CHARLES-HONORÉ (1779–1819) *New York cabinetmaker of the Federal era, whose designs were closely related to the French Empire style.*

MACKINTOSH, CHARLES RENNIE (1869–1928) *Scottish architect and designer, best known for his gently curving, elongated furniture in the Art Nouveau style.*

MAROT, DANIEL (1663–1752) *French-born Huguenot architect and designer who worked in Holland and England. His baroque style is characterized by elaborate carving and piercing.*

MORRIS, WILLIAM (1834–96) *Inspiration behind the Arts and Crafts movement. Morris advocated a return to the craftsmanship of the medieval era, praising simply made furniture and artefacts.*

PHYFE, DUNCAN (1768–1854) *New York cabinetmaker who introduced the Grecian ornaments that dominated the last 10 years of the American Federal period. A leading exponent of Directoire and Empire furniture.*

PUGIN, A.W.N. (1812–52) *Advocate of the Gothic revival whose influence extended until the 1880s; his principles and philosophy inspired many Arts and Crafts cabinetmakers.*

ROENTGEN, DAVID (1743–1807) *Son of Abraham Roentgen (1711–93), founder of the family furniture-making firm at Neuwied, Germany, in 1750. Roentgen developed the rococo style of his father, using rich carving and exotic inlays; later he switched to more rigid classical forms, often embellished with bronze appliqué.*

SCHINKEL, KARL FRIEDRICH (1781–1841) *A Berlin architect whose work greatly influenced the Biedermeier style.*

SHERATON, THOMAS (1751–1806) *English cabinetmaker who developed the neoclassical style in furniture; the style of refined elegance and balance is taken from his books* The Cabinet Dictionary *(1803) and* The Cabinet-Maker and Upholsterer's Drawing Book *(1791–94).*

STICKLEY, GUSTAVE (1857–1942) *New York cabinetmaker influenced by the Arts and Crafts movement who produced "Mission" furniture – simple rectilinear pieces, relieved only by slightly swelling legs or curved aprons.*

THONET BROTHERS *Austrian furniture-making firm established in 1842, which by 1871 was the largest such company in the world. Thonet specialized in mass-produced bentwood furniture (see Woods used for furniture), which was popular in Europe and the United States.*

VOYSEY, C.F.A. (1857–1941) *British architect, designer, and author best known for his contribution to Art Nouveau.*

WIENER WERKSTÄTTE *The "Vienna Workshops," a cooperative of Austrian craftsmen founded in 1903 by designers Josef Hoffman and Koloman Moser.*

WRIGHT, FRANK LLOYD (1867–1959) *American architect and design theorist whose organic approach to buildings, interiors, and furnishings made him a major influence in the American Arts and Crafts movement.*

Gadrooning

Lacquer

Papier-mâché

Patera

Trefoil

Vernis martin

Pieces of furniture

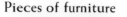

Architect's desk

Bergère

Cellaret

Loo table

APPRENTICE PIECE *Scaled-down piece made to prove an apprentice's craftsmanship before he started work on full-sized pieces.*

ARCHITECT'S DESK *A table or desk with a top hinged to provide a sloped working surface. See p. 123.*

ARMADA CHEST *Strong box of the 16th, 17th and 18th centuries, with heavy iron banding, false keyholes, looped hasps for padlocks, and an elaborate lock in the lid.*

ARMOIRE *French term for a large, tall cupboard or press used for storing clothes. See pp. 100–101 and 138–39.*

AUMBRY *Late-medieval food cupboard, often with a partially open top for ventilation.*

BACK STOOL *A three- or four-legged stool with a back, which evolved into an early form of side chair, so called because they had no arms. See p. 21.*

BALLOON-BACK CHAIR *Chair with an open O-shaped back and nipped waist. Popular as sets of dining chairs from the 1820s until 1900. See pp. 28–29.*

BERGÈRE *French upholstered armchair made from the 1720s. In the 19th century, this term was applied to an upholstered, deep-seated chair, with a loose cushion and padded arms joined to a sweeping back rail.*

BIBLE BOX *Oak box with a hinged lid used in the 17th century for storing the family Bible or writing implements and often a candle.*

BONHEUR DU JOUR *A lady's writing table, with shelves and pigeonholes, introduced in the 1760s. See p. 108.*

BREAKFAST TABLE *Small, four-legged table with two hinged flaps; easily moved.*

BUFFET *A side or serving table usually of two or more tiers, the function of which was replaced in the 18th century by the sideboard.*

BUREAU À CYLINDRE *Late 18th century desk with a curved lid that slides back beneath the top when opened. See p. 108.*

BUREAU PLAT *Flat-topped writing desk with drawers beneath. See pp. 116–17.*

CABINET *Cupboard with drawers and shelves for storage or display; often highly decorated. See pp. 76–91.*

CAMPAIGN CHEST *Intended for officers on active service, these had brass-bound corners, recessed handles, and detachable feet for ease of transportation. Typical features included drawers, a mirror, wash basin, and secretaire drawer.*

CANTERBURY *A 19th-century stand with compartments to hold music. See p. 147.*

CARTONNIER *French 18th-century cabinet, usually made as part of a set with a flat-topped desk, now often separated. See p. 117.*

CARVER *Dining chair with arms, which is also often called an elbow chair.*

CASSONE *Carved, gilded, or inlaid Italian dowry chest. See pp. 68–69.*

CELLARET *Lockable box for storing wine, either part of a sideboard or free standing. See pp. 150–51.*

CHAISE LONGUE *Upholstered, elongated chair with a complete or partial back. See pp. 34–35.*

CHEVAL *Tall, free-standing mirror or screen on a four-legged base. See p. 105.*

CHIFFONIER *In France, a tall chest of drawers popular in the mid- to late 18th century. In Britain, a form of cabinet with cupboards and a sideboard top, often used as a sideboard in the dining room.*

COASTER *Circular stand with a raised silver rim or gallery, used for port or wine bottles on the table, introduced in the 1760s.*

COMMODE *French term for a chest of drawers or cabinet, often highly decorated with veneers and metal mounts. Also a bedside cupboard containing a chamber pot. See pp. 72–73.*

CORNER CHAIR *Early Georgian chair with two side legs, one front, and one back leg, which fits neatly into a corner; also known as a writing chair. See p. 25.*

CREDENZA *Sideboard with doors, often topped with drawers.*

CURULE *An X-framed, often folding chair or stool, popular during the late 18th and 19th century classical revivals. See p. 27.*

DAVENPORT *Small writing desk consisting of a sloping top, often with drawers that open from the side. See p. 122–23.*

DAYBED *Upholstered couch with a slanting backrest used for resting during the day.*

DROP-LEAF TABLE *The surface area of such tables can be increased by raising an extra leaf, supported on hinged legs or arms or brackets. See pp. 44 and 48–49.*

DRUM TABLE *Circular table with a deep frieze containing drawers.*

ENCOIGNURE *French free-standing cupboard, often with a marble top. See p. 91.*

FAUTEUIL A LA REINE *A large, flat-backed 18th-century French armchair.*

GATE-LEG TABLE *One in which a pivoting leg supports a hinged leaf or flap. See pp. 44 and 48–49.*

GUÉRIDON *A candlestand. See pp. 60–61.*

HADLEY CHEST *An elaborately carved dowry chest, originating in Hadley, Mass., in the 17th century. See p. 144–45.*

HUTCH *Large tablelike top with cupboards or drawers beneath and open shelves above on which to display tableware. See pp. 83 and 132–33.*

HOOPBACK CHAIR *Chairs whose top rail and uprights form a continuous curve.*

KLISMOS *Classical Greek saber-legged chair with forward-curving front legs and back-curving back ones. See p. 27.*

LADDERBACK CHAIR *Chair with horizontal rails or slats.*

LOO TABLE *Usually circular games table, originally for playing the game lanterloo.*

PIER GLASS *Mirror designed to hang between two windows, often above a pier or console table.*

PRIE DIEU *Low-seated high-backed chair on which to kneel for prayers. See p. 149.*

SCONCE *Wall light consisting of a backplate and candle holders.*

SECRÉTAIRE À ABATTANT *Tall French writing desk, usually with a drop front. See pp. 108 and 110–11.*

SEMAINIER *French linen chest, usually with seven drawers. See p. 71.*

SETTLE *Bench with a high back and arms and sometimes a chest for storage under the seat; popular in the 16th to 19th centuries.*

SOCIABLE *Upholstered S-shaped sofa with swivel ends so that occupants could face each other for intimate conversation.*

TABOURET *A low upholstered French stool of the 17th to 18th centuries. See p. 27.*

TESTER *Originally the canopy or ceiling of a large bed, now synonymous with four poster. See pp. 94 and 96–97.*

TORCHÈRE *A stand for a candle or lamp. Smaller types are portable. See pp. 60–61.*

URN TABLE *Small 18th-century table designed to hold a water urn or kettle.*

VARGUENO *16th-century Spanish writing desk consisting of a rectangular chest, with a drop front and drawers inside, which sits on a stand. See p. 87.*

WELLINGTON CHEST *Narrow early 19th-century chest with 6 to 12 shallow drawers and a lockable securing flap.*

WINDSOR CHAIR *A type of wooden chair with a spindle back. See pp. 130–31.*

WING CHAIR *Upholstered chair with a high back and projecting wing pieces at each side. See pp. 35 and 40–41.*

WRITING SLOPE *A robust wooden box often with brass corners or edges, and a hinged top that opens to form a writing surface.*

Cabinetmaking terminology

NOTE: This list details general terms relating to the way furniture is constructed. Terms relating to specific pieces are described and illustrated at the beginning of each chapter. See pp. 16–19, 34–37, 42–45, 64–67, 76–79, 92–95, 106–109, and 124–27.

BACKBOARD *The unpolished back of a piece of wall furniture or a framed mirror, not designed to be seen.*

BAIL HANDLE *The shaped bar of a looped drop handle, anchored at both ends.*

BENDS *A rocking chair's curved runners.*

BLOCKFRONT *Construction technique used on case furniture usually consisting of three vertical panels, the outer two convex and the center one concave.*

BOW FRONT *A curving, convex front on a chest of drawers, lowboy, or sideboard.*

BREAKFRONT *Protruding center section on a piece of furniture such as a bookcase or sideboard, popular in the 18th century.*

CANDLE SLIDE *Retractable wooden support for a candle found on 18th-century bureau-bookcases.*

CANTED CORNER *Slanting, chamfered, or beveled edge.*

CARCASS *The main structure of a piece of furniture excluding drawers, doors, and the like.*

CASE FURNITURE *A piece designed to contain something.*

CHAMFER *An angle on the edge of a piece of wood, achieved by planing or cutting.*

DOVETAIL *Close-fitting joint with interlocking tenons used in the making of high-quality furniture.*

DOWEL *Wooden "pin" used to secure a joint; also a peg securing a mortise and tenon joints. Hand-cut until about 1850.*

ÉBÉNISTE *French term for a cabinetmaker specializing in veneering.*

MENUISIER *French carpenter making carved wood furniture such as chairs.*

MITER *The diagonal joint where two moldings meet at right angles.*

MORTISE AND TENON JOINT *Introduced in the 16th century, this involves cutting a hole (the mortise) into one piece of wood into which the projecting tenon from a second piece fits snugly. The joint may also be glued and/or pegged with a dowel.*

MUNTIN *The vertical framework between panels. See also stile.*

PEGGED FURNITURE *Early tables and chests which could be dismantled simply by removing the pegs that held them together.*

PLINTH *A solid base section used instead of legs on cabinet furniture.*

RABBET *Groove, channel, or recess cut along the edge of a piece of wood to receive the end or edge of another piece of wood, as in drawers.*

RE-ENTRANT CORNER *A shaped indentation at the corner of a table.*

RUNNER *Piece of wood along which a corresponding groove in a drawer side slides; some runners were fitted to the drawer bottom.*

STILE *Vertical member of a framework placed at the end or corner of a piece of paneled furniture.*

STRAP HINGE *Hinge with a long arm, used in the 16th and early 17th centuries.*

Woods used for furniture

ACACIA *Yellow hardwood with brown veins used for banding and inlays.*

ALDER *A wood popular for country furniture since it turns well.*

AMBOYNA *Red-brown East Indian wood used for veneers and inlay in the 18th and 19th centuries.*

ASH *A close-grained wood resembling oak, ash was popular for country furniture and for drawer linings.*

BAMBOO *Tropical grass with a cream-colored hollow jointed stem. Used for furniture and often imitated.*

BEECH *An inexpensive hardwood often used to make chair frames and country furniture.*

BENTWOOD *Lightweight or laminated wood that has been bent into curved shapes by steaming or soaking in hot water.*

BIRCH *Close-grained yellow wood used for chairs and case furniture.*

BIRD'S-EYE MAPLE *Pale wood in which the grain forms rings around small dark knots; popular for veneers.*

BOXWOOD *Yellow close-grained hardwood used for marquetry in the 16th to 17th centuries, and stringing in the late 18th and early 19th.*

BURL WALNUT *A veneer cut from a cross-section of the gnarled grain at a tree's base.*

CALAMANDER *Reddish-brown hardwood used for veneer and crossbanding.*

CEDAR *Popular for American carcasses in the 18th and 19th centuries. Its long-lasting fragrance was believed to repel moths.*

CHESTNUT *A wood that matures to a rich reddish brown, particularly popular in southern Europe.*

EBONIZED WOOD *Wood, often of poor quality, that is stained and polished to resemble ebony.*

EBONY *Used for both inlay and veneering from the 17th century.*

ELM *Light brown wood with a strong grain used for country chairs.*

FRUITWOOD *The wood of any fruit-bearing trees such as apple, cherry, plum, or pear. Good for carving and easy to turn.*

KINGWOOD *Purplish South American wood used for veneer.*

LABURNUM *A yellowish wood with dark veins used mainly for veneers.*

MAHOGANY *Rich copper-red wood from Central and South America, popular from the 1730s on.*

MAPLE *Pale wood with a darker, wavy grain used in North American furniture and also exported.*

OAK *The most popular wood for furniture until the mid-17th century, and used thereafter in country and provincial furniture. It has a strong grain that darkens with age to finish from pale brown to almost black. Bog oak is taken from parts of the tree that have been submerged in a peat bog and is black.*

PADOUK *A dark hardwood used both solid and for veneers.*

PINE *A softwood used until the early 20th century for making cheaper furniture and for the frames and carcasses of more expensive pieces. Pine pieces were often painted.*

ROSEWOOD *Dark purple-brown wood from India and Brazil used as a veneer from the late 18th century.*

SATINWOOD *Prized in the late 18th century for its dense grain and yellow color, satinwood was used solid and for veneers.*

SYCAMORE *Close-grained pale wood used mainly for veneer, but also stained green and known as harewood.*

TULIPWOOD *Pinkish hardwood native to Central and South America, used for veneer, inlay, and banding.*

WALNUT *Favored from the mid-17th to early 18th century for fine furniture, walnut has a faint grain and coarse, scattered pores. It varies in color from light to dark brown.*

YEW *Pale wood hard to work but easy to steam, so used for the hooped backs of country chairs; burr yew was used for veneers.*

ZEBRAWOOD *Dark South American wood with distinctive black and white stripes.*

Applewood and pearwood caddies

Birch frame

Bird's-eye maple

Ebonized wood

Burr walnut

PERIODS AND STYLES

	16 00		16 50			17 00	
STYLE	GOTHIC (TO 1620)	BAROQUE (1620–1700)				ROCOCO (1700–60)	
GREAT BRITAIN AND IRELAND	JACOBEAN	CAROLEAN	COMMONWEALTH	RESTORATION	WILLIAM & MARY	QUEEN ANNE	EARLY GEORGIAN
UNITED STATES	EARLY COLONIAL (TO 1700)				WILLIAM & MARY STYLE (1700–25)	QUEEN ANNE STYLE (1725–55)	
FRANCE	HENRI IV (1589–1610)	LOUIS XIII (1610–43)				RÉGENCE (1715–23)	
NORTHERN EUROPE	RENAISSANCE (TO 1650)		BAROQUE (1650–1730)			ROCOCO (1700–60)	
MEDITERRANEAN EUROPE	RENAISSANCE (TO 1650) MANNERISM (ITALY) MOORISH INFLUENCE (SPAIN)		BAROQUE (1650–1730) CHURRIQUERESQUE (SPAIN)			ROCOCO (1700–60)	

16 00   16 50   17 00

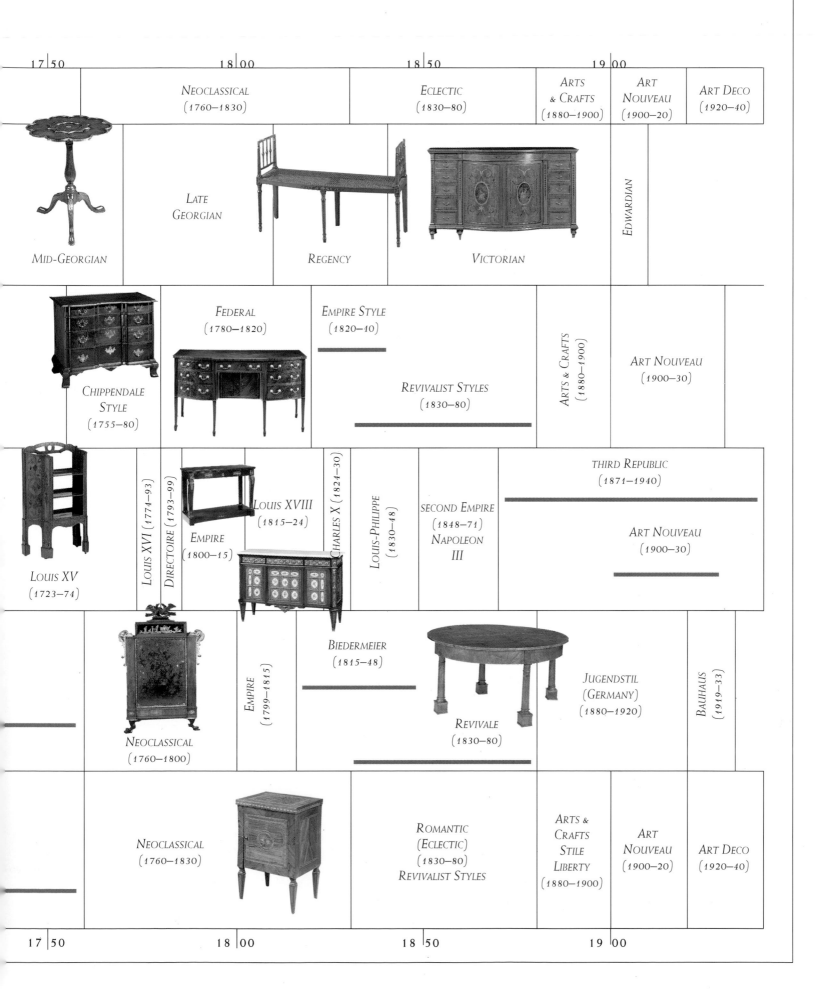

17 50   18 00   18 50   19 00

NEOCLASSICAL
(1760–1830)

ECLECTIC
(1830–80)

ARTS
& CRAFTS
(1880–1900)

ART
NOUVEAU
(1900–20)

ART DECO
(1920–40)

LATE
GEORGIAN

MID-GEORGIAN

REGENCY

VICTORIAN

EDWARDIAN

FEDERAL
(1780–1820)

EMPIRE STYLE
(1820–10)

ARTS & CRAFTS
(1880–1900)

ART NOUVEAU
(1900–30)

CHIPPENDALE
STYLE
(1755–80)

REVIVALIST STYLES
(1830–80)

LOUIS XVI (1774–93)

DIRECTOIRE (1793–99)

CHARLES X (1824–30)

LOUIS XVIII
(1815–24)

THIRD REPUBLIC
(1871–1940)

LOUIS-PHILIPPE
(1830–48)

SECOND EMPIRE
(1848–71)
NAPOLEON
III

ART NOUVEAU
(1900–30)

EMPIRE
(1800–15)

LOUIS XV
(1723–74)

BIEDERMEIER
(1815–48)

EMPIRE
(1799–1815)

JUGENDSTIL
(GERMANY)
(1880–1920)

BAUHAUS
(1919–33)

REVIVALE
(1830–80)

NEOCLASSICAL
(1760–1800)

NEOCLASSICAL
(1760–1830)

ROMANTIC
(ECLECTIC)
(1830–80)
REVIVALIST STYLES

ARTS &
CRAFTS
STILE
LIBERTY
(1880–1900)

ART
NOUVEAU
(1900–20)

ART DECO
(1920–40)

17 50   18 00   18 50   19 00

CABINETMAKERS AND DESIGNERS

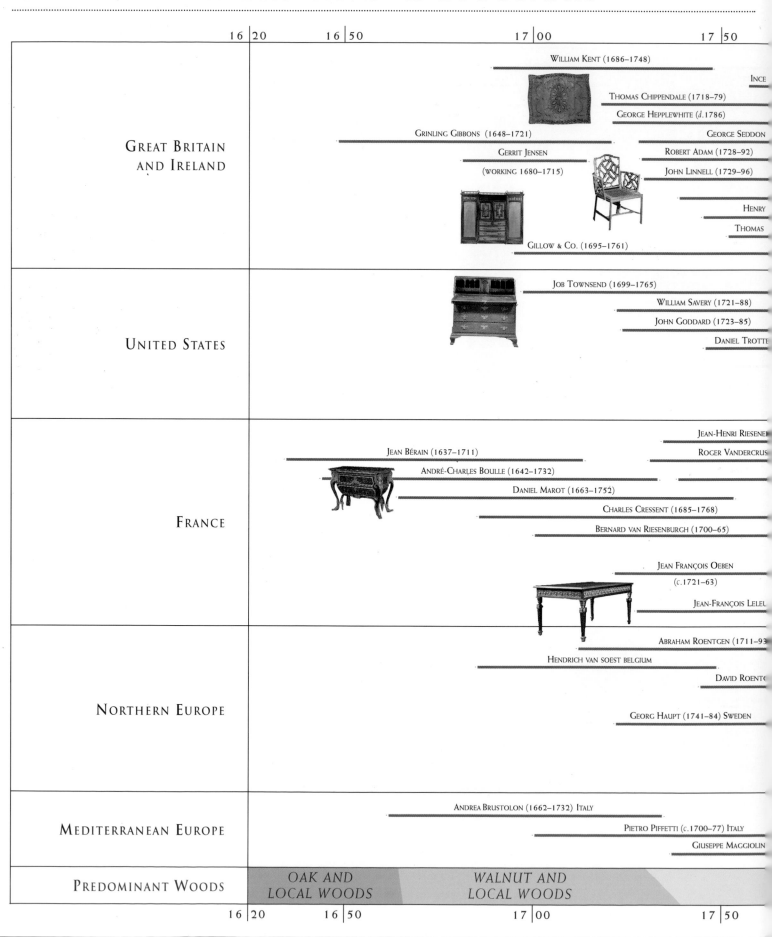

	16|20	16|50	17|00	17|50
GREAT BRITAIN AND IRELAND			WILLIAM KENT (1686–1748)	INCE
				THOMAS CHIPPENDALE (1718–79)
				GEORGE HEPPLEWHITE (*d.*1786)
			GRINLING GIBBONS (1648–1721)	GEORGE SEDDON
			GERRIT JENSEN	ROBERT ADAM (1728–92)
			(WORKING 1680–1715)	JOHN LINNELL (1729–96)
				HENRY
				THOMAS
			GILLOW & CO. (1695–1761)	
UNITED STATES			JOB TOWNSEND (1699–1765)	
				WILLIAM SAVERY (1721–88)
				JOHN GODDARD (1723–85)
				DANIEL TROTTE
FRANCE				JEAN-HENRI RIESENE
		JEAN BÉRAIN (1637–1711)		ROGER VANDERCRUS
		ANDRÉ-CHARLES BOULLE (1642–1732)		
		DANIEL MAROT (1663–1752)		
			CHARLES CRESSENT (1685–1768)	
			BERNARD VAN RIESENBURGH (1700–65)	
				JEAN FRANÇOIS OEBEN
				(c.1721–63)
				JEAN-FRANÇOIS LELEU
NORTHERN EUROPE				ABRAHAM ROENTGEN (1711–93
			HENDRICH VAN SOEST BELGIUM	
				DAVID ROENTG
			GEORG HAUPT (1741–84) SWEDEN	
MEDITERRANEAN EUROPE			ANDREA BRUSTOLON (1662–1732) ITALY	
				PIETRO PIFFETTI (c.1700–77) ITALY
				GIUSEPPE MAGGIOLIN
PREDOMINANT WOODS	OAK AND LOCAL WOODS		WALNUT AND LOCAL WOODS	
	16|20	16|50	17|00	17|50

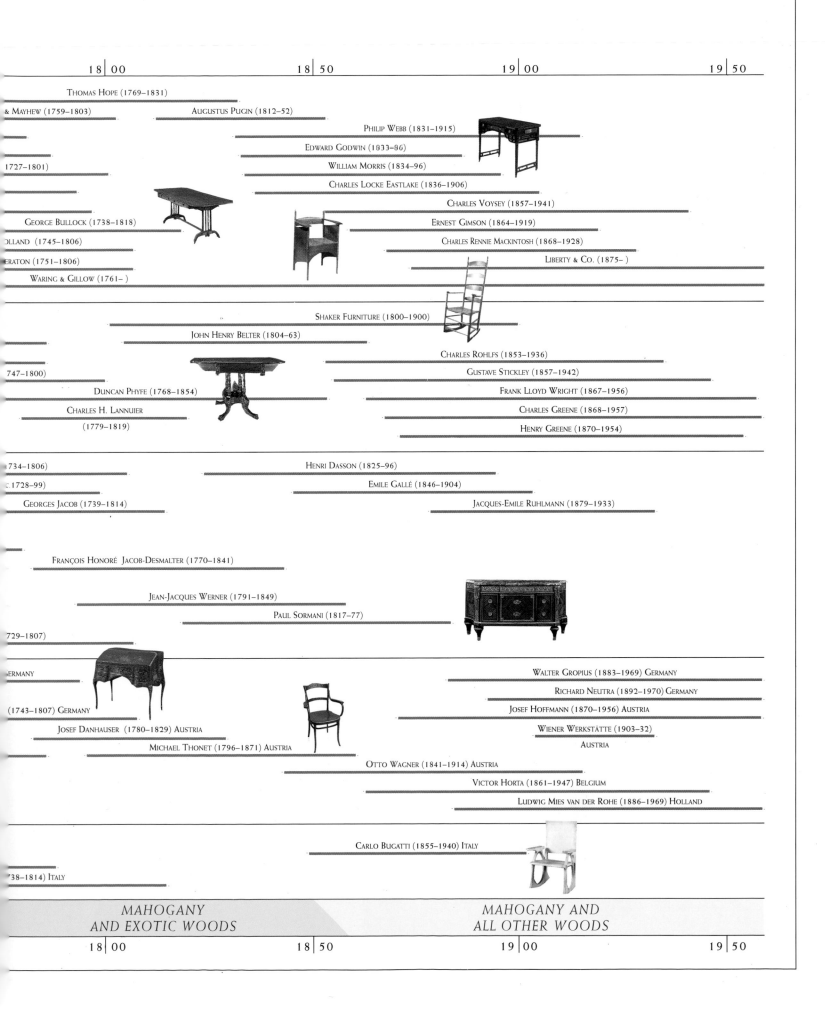

| | 18 00 | | 18 50 | | 19 00 | | 19 50 |

THOMAS HOPE (1769–1831)

& MAYHEW (1759–1803)   AUGUSTUS PUGIN (1812–52)

PHILIP WEBB (1831–1915)

EDWARD GODWIN (1833–86)

1727–1801)   WILLIAM MORRIS (1834–96)

CHARLES LOCKE EASTLAKE (1836–1906)

CHARLES VOYSEY (1857–1941)

GEORGE BULLOCK (1738–1818)   ERNEST GIMSON (1864–1919)

OLLAND (1745–1806)   CHARLES RENNIE MACKINTOSH (1868–1928)

ERATON (1751–1806)   LIBERTY & CO. (1875–)

WARING & GILLOW (1761–)

SHAKER FURNITURE (1800–1900)

JOHN HENRY BELTER (1804–63)

CHARLES ROHLFS (1853–1936)

747–1800)   GUSTAVE STICKLEY (1857–1942)

DUNCAN PHYFE (1768–1854)   FRANK LLOYD WRIGHT (1867–1956)

CHARLES H. LANNUIER   CHARLES GREENE (1868–1957)

(1779–1819)   HENRY GREENE (1870–1954)

1734–1806)   HENRI DASSON (1825–96)

1728–99)   EMILE GALLÉ (1846–1904)

GEORGES JACOB (1739–1814)   JACQUES-EMILE RUHLMANN (1879–1933)

FRANÇOIS HONORÉ JACOB-DESMALTER (1770–1841)

JEAN-JACQUES WERNER (1791–1849)

PAUL SORMANI (1817–77)

729–1807)

ERMANY   WALTER GROPIUS (1883–1969) GERMANY

RICHARD NEUTRA (1892–1970) GERMANY

(1743–1807) GERMANY   JOSEF HOFFMANN (1870–1956) AUSTRIA

JOSEF DANHAUSER (1780–1829) AUSTRIA   WIENER WERKSTÄTTE (1903–32)

MICHAEL THONET (1796–1871) AUSTRIA   AUSTRIA

OTTO WAGNER (1841–1914) AUSTRIA

VICTOR HORTA (1861–1947) BELGIUM

LUDWIG MIES VAN DER ROHE (1886–1969) HOLLAND

CARLO BUGATTI (1855–1940) ITALY

738–1814) ITALY

| *MAHOGANY* | | | | *MAHOGANY AND* | | |
| *AND EXOTIC WOODS* | | | | *ALL OTHER WOODS* | | |

| | 18 00 | | 18 50 | | 19 00 | | 19 50 |

OTHER USEFUL TERMS

BALUSTER A vase-shaped column of wood, usually turned, sometimes used in chair legs. Some splats are also of baluster form.

CHAMFER See pp. 8–11.

EAR PIECE A decorative piece of wood that is either glued to the knee of a cabriole leg or that projects from each end of the top rail.

FINIAL A decorative ornament found on the top of the uprights of some chair backs. See also pp. 106–7.

FRAME A chair's basic structural components.

MONOPODIUM A leg shaped to resemble an animal's head and leg (see pp. 26–27).

SHOE-PIECE The shaped projection above the seat rail that houses the base of the splat.

STILE The vertical piece of a chair frame adjoining the top rail. See also BACK UPRIGHT.

TURNING See pp. 126–27.

YOKE Another name for the top rail.

CANEWORK BACK
Backs of chairs became higher from about 1660, to support the sitter's head. Cane was introduced into Europe in the 1660s by the Dutch and English East India companies.

BACK UPRIGHT
A vertical piece of wood that continues the line of the back legs.

SPLAT
The central upright of a wooden chair back, rising from the seat to the top rail.

SEAT
Used imprecisely to mean a chair, settee, or stool, the seat is technically the part of a chair on which to sit. It is supported by the seat rail and legs.

SCROLLED ARM
One of the most popular types of arm in the 17th century. This one has japanned decoration, the European imitation of oriental lacquer.

APRON
The shaped front and/or side edge of a chair; the term is also used to describe the edge below a table top or drawer line.

SEAT RAIL
The horizontal rail that supports the seat of a chair.

CABRIOLE LEG
This is an early type of cabriole leg, which developed toward the end of the 17th century and was popular for much of the 18th and again in the 19th.

STRETCHER
A horizontal strut or rail between the legs of a chair or table.

CHAIRS & STOOLS

Essentially seats with backs and four legs intended for one person, chairs are so common today that they are taken for granted. Although they have been used for perhaps 5,000 years, they only started to become ubiquitous pieces of furniture about 350 years ago, when they ceased to be regarded primarily as symbols of rank.

This ubiquity has meant that there is an enormous variation in the size and shape of chairs. At one end of the scale are simple wooden hall chairs, intended to be sat on for only a few minutes at a time by visitors wearing outdoor clothes. At the other are those designed for sumptuous dining rooms, where guests lingered for hours on beautifully carved chairs with deep, padded seats. Chairs have been made by country carpenters and turners and by the world's best-known cabinetmakers; most are wooden, but they also exist in metal and even paper; they have been painted, lacquered, and gilded; they may be innovative or faithful reproductions – or elements of both these extremes. Above all, they have been – and still are – practical, which is why antique chairs and stools continue to be so popular in the salesroom.

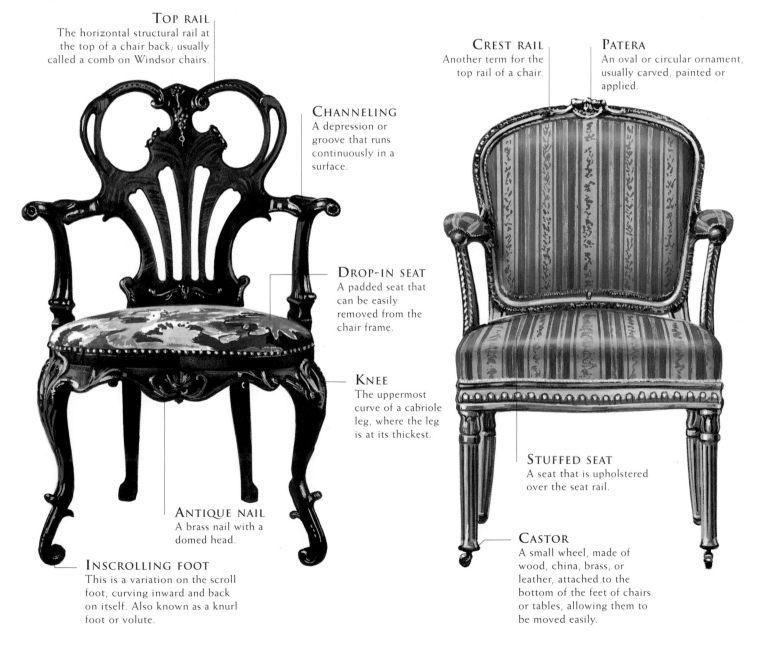

TOP RAIL
The horizontal structural rail at the top of a chair back; usually called a comb on Windsor chairs.

CHANNELING
A depression or groove that runs continuously in a surface.

DROP-IN SEAT
A padded seat that can be easily removed from the chair frame.

KNEE
The uppermost curve of a cabriole leg, where the leg is at its thickest.

ANTIQUE NAIL
A brass nail with a domed head.

INSCROLLING FOOT
This is a variation on the scroll foot, curving inward and back on itself. Also known as a knurl foot or volute.

CREST RAIL
Another term for the top rail of a chair.

PATERA
An oval or circular ornament, usually carved, painted or applied.

STUFFED SEAT
A seat that is upholstered over the seat rail.

CASTOR
A small wheel, made of wood, china, brass, or leather, attached to the bottom of the feet of chairs or tables, allowing them to be moved easily.

DESIGN DETAILS

Although the basic construction methods used in chair making have not altered greatly over the past 200 years, it is still possible to identify when a chair was made by analyzing its parts. The shape and decoration of a chair's back, splat, legs, and feet usually reflect the styling of the age in which it was made, so looking carefully at these elements can help you to establish a date. If you know what should be found on a period chair, it is relatively simple to identify reproductions and later revivals. Reproductions, in particular, often differ in size from the chairs they copy, and any carving or other decoration is too elaborate and incorporates too many different features.

These illustrations provide a visual reference to many of the most distinctive features of a chair.

Construction of drop-in seat blocks and shoe-pieces

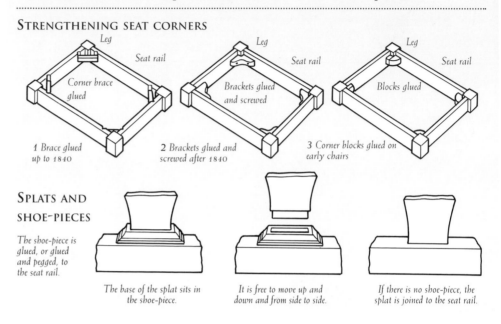

STRENGTHENING SEAT CORNERS

1 Brace glued up to 1840

2 Brackets glued and screwed after 1840

3 Corner blocks glued on early chairs

SPLATS AND SHOE-PIECES

The shoe-piece is glued, or glued and pegged, to the seat rail.

The base of the splat sits in the shoe-piece.

It is free to move up and down and from side to side.

If there is no shoe-piece, the splat is joined to the seat rail.

Legs

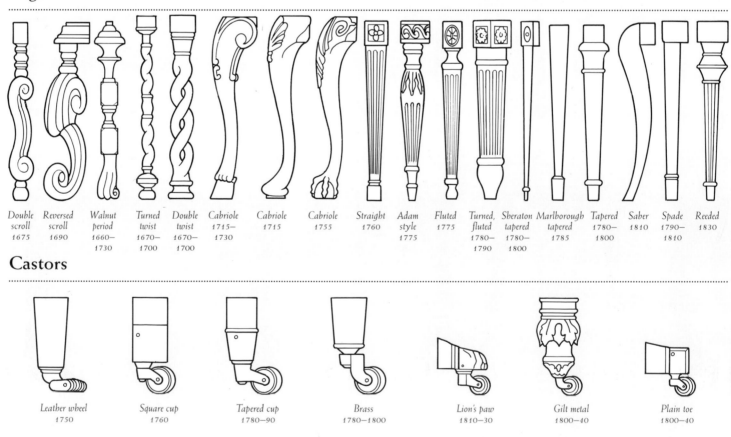

Double scroll 1675 | Reversed scroll 1690 | Walnut period 1660–1730 | Turned twist 1670–1700 | Double twist 1670–1700 | Cabriole 1715–1730 | Cabriole 1715 | Cabriole 1755 | Straight 1760 | Adam style 1775 | Fluted 1775 | Turned, fluted 1780–1790 | Sheraton tapered 1780–1800 | Marlborough tapered 1785 | Tapered 1780–1800 | Saber 1810 | Spade 1790–1810 | Reeded 1830

Castors

Leather wheel 1750 | Square cup 1760 | Tapered cup 1780–90 | Brass 1780–1800 | Lion's paw 1810–30 | Gilt metal 1800–40 | Plain toe 1800–40

Stretchers

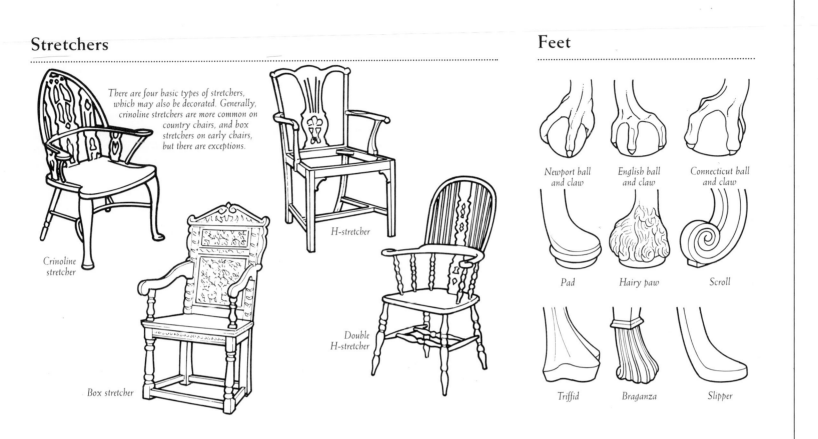

There are four basic types of stretchers, which may also be decorated. Generally, crinoline stretchers are more common on country chairs, and box stretchers on early chairs, but there are exceptions.

Crinoline stretcher

H-stretcher

Double H-stretcher

Box stretcher

Feet

Newport ball and claw

English ball and claw

Connecticut ball and claw

Pad

Hairy paw

Scroll

Triffid

Braganza

Slipper

Chair backs

Pilgrim slat
1680–1720

Waved slat or ladderback
1720 onward

Fiddleback
1720

Banister
1750–80

Chippendale ribband
1754

Chippendale Chinese style
1754

Studded leather
1775–1800

Federal oval
1790–1800

Hepplewhite shield
1794

Hepplewhite shield
1794

Hepplewhite square
1794

Sheraton parlor chair
1802

Sheraton parlor chair
1802

Sheraton parlor chair
1802

Sheraton parlor chair
1802

Sheraton parlor chair
1802

Sheraton parlor chair
1802

Sheraton parlor chair
1802

Sheraton shield
1802

Sheraton parlor chair
1802

Sheraton square
1800–10

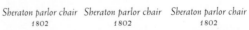

Sheraton square
1800–10

Rococo revival
1850–80

Renaissance revival
1860–1900

EARLY CHAIRS

In the Middle Ages, the most common forms of seating were stools and benches, usually trestle type. Chairs, which were regarded as a sign of rank, were reserved for the master and mistress of the house. These early chairs were of boxed, joined construction, but by the mid-16th century their design had evolved to lose the box panels under the seat and arms; since they bore a resemblance to wainscot paneling, such chairs were known as wainscot chairs. By this time, stools were also of joined construction, a style which remained popular well into the 17th century.

By the early 17th century, a lighter, more portable type of chair known as a back stool – literally a stool with a half back – had emerged. But chairs were by no means common until the middle years of the century.

After the restoration of the English monarchy in 1660, continental influences, especially French and Dutch (Charles II had spent many years of exile in Holland), increasingly affected chair designs. High backs and twisted and turned uprights and stretchers – including arched front stretchers – grew in popularity. The S-scroll became an important feature in leg design. Walnut and beech were the most common woods, and many chairs had cane upholstery, using cane imported from Malaya by the Dutch and English East India companies. The designs of Frenchman Daniel Marot, who worked in both Holland and England, influenced the style of carving on many chairs.

By the early 18th century, the design of chairs had evolved even further with the introduction of the hoop-shaped back with a vase-shaped splat, cabriole legs – which derived from S-scrolls – and serpentine curves. All of these are typical of chairs defined as being of Queen Anne style.

JACOBEAN OAK ARMCHAIR

Carved decorative finials; some chairs have "ear pieces" here.

Naturalistically carved S-scrolls; on Victorian copies, the carving is less crisp.

Scrolled arms with turned supports. There should be wear and a rich patina at the end of the arms through years of use.

The line of the arm supports and legs is often continuous.

Gadrooning, here carved on to the edge of the seat, was a common form of decoration on Elizabethan furniture and endured into the Victorian age.

Top rail with typical carving of stylized flower heads. The guilloche motif derived from classical architecture remained popular through the 18th century and into the 19th. Waved and scrolled cresting finishes the top of the rail.

PURITAN CHAIR

Dating from about 1655, this typically austere back stool has simple knob-turned decoration on the front legs and stretcher, and leather upholstery held by brass nails. Leather deteriorates with age, so is rare on chairs from this period.

Back panel, inlaid with holly and bog oak in a geometric design. The carved initials S.F.E., in common with most carved initials and dates, are a later addition. The back panel may well have come from another piece of furniture or paneling. Later additions are obvious from differences in coloration, but a contemporary piece of wood can be more difficult to spot.

LATE 17TH-CENTURY FLEMISH OPEN ARMCHAIR

The high back, scrolling arms, and turned legs and stretchers are typical of chairs found both in Britain and on the European mainland in this period. The fabric upholstery is contemporary, but the bun feet are later additions. Since feet are vulnerable, this is common; a chair with its original feet is worth more.

Turned baluster legs at the front, with plain ones at the rear are typical. Treat four matching legs with suspicion.

Box stretchers. On a genuine chair there will be wear only on the front stretcher from people's feet. If all the stretchers show signs of wear, the chair is probably a copy. All the feet, however, should show signs of wear.

QUEEN ANNE WALNUT CHAIR

The period described as Queen Anne in the United States lasted from about 1725 to 1755. This chair was made in Philadelphia in about 1740. It has a scrolling crest rail above a vase-shaped splat, and its cabriole legs end in pad feet. Walnut was the preferred wood in this period, although maple, cherry, and cedar were also used; mahogany became popular in the second half of the century.

THE RISE OF MAHOGANY

By the 1730s, walnut, the most popular wood for furniture since the 1660s, was becoming scarce. A succession of harsh winters had prompted the French – one of Europe's major producers – to ban its export in 1720. Helped by a reduction in import tariffs in 1733, mahogany from the West Indies became the predominant wood used in making furniture.

While chair styles of the early years of the century remained popular, gradual changes were introduced. Backs became lower, and cabriole legs, now with hipped knees, became thicker and often ended in ball and claw feet. Splats were pierced and wider at the top than before; shoe-pieces were introduced in the early 18th century.

Thomas Chippendale's *The Gentleman and Cabinet Maker's Director* of 1754 showed, among other things, new designs for chairs with both upholstered and wonderfully carved backs in a variety of styles, including rococo, chinoiserie, and Gothic. Some of his designs, as in much of Europe, were influenced by French taste. In France, chairs played an important role in the furnishing of rooms with two types common: those described as *meublant* were placed against the walls of a room, while the smaller and more portable *courant* were used in the center. Stools were still being made, usually as part of a set of furniture; they stood either against a wall or in a window embrasure.

Interest in the Gothic style developed in the second half of the 18th century, and some grand houses, such as Strawberry Hill on the outskirts of London, were decorated entirely in this style. However, many chairs that are called Gothic are in fact classical in origin, although they are decorated with Gothic motifs and ornament.

GEORGE III MAHOGANY OPEN ARMCHAIR

Fretwork carving on the stiles. Such carving on later copies is generally much heavier and more ornate.

The outcurved arms have downswept supports.

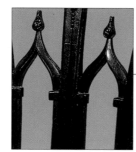

Carved and pierced splat with Gothic arches.

Screws were countersunk and hidden from view by wooden plugs in the 18th century.

The cabriole legs, here ending in scroll toes, have the correct elegant proportions: on copies they are usually too thin.

The seat of an armchair is always a little wider than that of a chair without arms. If the seats in a set are all the same width, this indicates that arms have been added to make two armchairs. Seats are narrower and seat rails thinner on reproductions.

The serpentine top rail, here with carved foliage, is typical, as is the lower back. Never lift a chair by its back or arms, since this can cause damage.

Arm supports end about a third of the way back from the chair front. Arms began to "creep away" from the front of the chair during the Queen Anne period, gradually receding to these proportions.

The shoe-piece was carved from a separate piece of wood and attached to the seat rail; a shoe-piece that forms part of the rail indicates that the chair dates from a later period.

The curve on the back legs is usually stronger on copies.

Stuffed and drop-in seats are found on such chairs. To tell if a chair is period or not, remove the drop-in seat and lift the chair. If it is heavy, the chair is 18th century; if the frame is light, it is a later copy.

CHIPPENDALE WALNUT CHAIR

American cabinetmakers at first followed Chippendale's designs, but they were soon incorporating native motifs. On this chair, made in about 1760 in Philadelphia, the crest rail has a central shell carving; carved shells adorn the "ear pieces" covering its fluted stiles; and the seat rail has a shell carved at its center. The splat is also heavily carved with scrolling foliage. The cabriole legs end in ball and claw feet.

GEORGE II BLACK AND GILT ARMCHAIR

This chinoiserie open armchair is part of a suite of japanned furniture made for the Chinese bedroom at Badminton House, Gloucestershire, in 1752–54. The chairs have been redecorated, but still bear traces of their original red, blue, and gilt decoration. Original decoration in good condition is a bonus, but these traces add to the historical interest of the chair and do not adversely affect value.

GEORGE III RIBBAND-BACK SIDE CHAIR

One of a pair, this chair is made to one of the three designs for ribband-back chairs featured in the first (1754) edition of the *Director*. Chippendale derived these designs from the work of of Jean Bérain and the chair is a fine example of his interpretation of the French rococo style. Carvers were also made to ribband-back designs.

NEOCLASSICAL ERA

Inspired by the excavations at Pompeii and Herculaneum, neoclassicism had, by the 1770s, emerged to become the dominant architectural style in Europe. In Britain the foremost exponent of this style was Robert Adam, who designed every element of his interiors, even handles, keyplates, and other door hardware. His designs, incorporating the restrained use of classical motifs such as anthemions, ram's heads, and paterae, influenced both furniture designers and cabinetmakers.

Thomas Chippendale, among others, made furniture for some of Adam's refurbishments, including Harewood House and Nostell Priory, both in Yorkshire. Some of Adam's chairs owe a great deal to the Louis XVI style of such *menuisiers* as Georges Jacob, but they are lighter and usually feature either oval or rectangular backs.

Adam's influence is apparent in the designs of George Hepplewhite, whose *Cabinetmaker and Upholsterer's Guide* was published in 1788, two years after his death. The chairs it illustrates have a light simplicity, with surface ornament and painting replacing the heavier carved decoration of earlier periods. Many chairs had shield-shaped backs with splats in the form of wheat sheaves, Prince-of-Wales feathers, or lyres. Legs were straight and tapered, usually into spade feet.

The designs of Thomas Sheraton, a furniture designer rather than maker, were even lighter in appearance than those of Hepplewhite and featured chairs with molded or reeded tapering legs with spade feet. Some of his inspiration derived from France where, by the end of the century, ancient Greek and Roman designs were influencing furniture in what became known as the Directoire style.

GEORGE III GILTWOOD OPEN ARMCHAIR

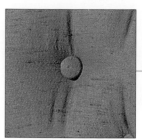

The buttoned back is padded and cushioned. Such chairs are of limited use if they are uncomfortable, so buttoning is often replaced.

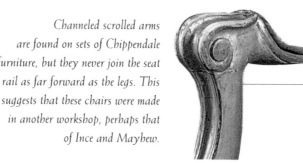

Channeled scrolled arms are found on sets of Chippendale furniture, but they never join the seat rail as far forward as the legs. This suggests that these chairs were made in another workshop, perhaps that of Ince and Mayhew.

Changes in fashion meant that the arms once more came almost to the front of the chair.

The seat rail is fluted, centered at the front by a patera. Seat-rail sides at this time often curved in toward the back of the chair.

The chair has been regilded, which is not unusual given normal wear. But it is still possible — and much more desirable — to find a chair with its original decoration.

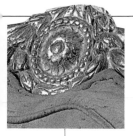

Channeled inverted-heart-shaped back with a husk-festooned patera. Shoe-pieces were not used on chairs with oval backs. The back joins the back legs above the seat rail.

CHINESE EXPORT LACQUER CHAIR

Made in the Hepplewhite style, this chair has a typical shield back and shaped splat, here with a triple leaf design, downswept arms, and square tapering legs. The drop-in seat is a later addition: the original would have been caned. It may only be possible to tell this from underneath: there will be cane holes on the underside of the frame.

GEORGE III MAHOGANY CORNER ARMCHAIR

Corner chairs first made an appearance in the early 18th century when they were probably used as writing chairs. Their basic design remained relatively unchanged until Victorian times, although decoration followed the styles of the day. Edwardian revivals also exist.

GEORGE III OPEN ARMCHAIR

One of a set of four dating from the 1780s, this chair may have been made by Thomas Chippendale the Younger. It is in the Louis XVI "antique" style, with molded fluted frame, fluted legs, and carved leaf decoration headed by demi-paterae. Although made only a few years later than the annotated chair, it has clearly lighter, more elegant proportions. The decoration reflects the vogue created by Hepplewhite.

Retipped leg: this may affect value, depending on the extent of other restoration.

Fluted tapering leg. Square tapering legs taper on the inside edge only.

REGENCY AND EMPIRE STYLES

As interest in earlier civilizations grew in the first years of the 19th century, ancient Egypt became as important a source of inspiration as the already popular Greece and Rome. The influence of the Greek klismos chair is apparent in many Regency chairs, both in direct copies and in scroll-backed, saber-legged dining chairs. But the lightness of the last decades of the 18th century was lost as chairs became more solid in appearance. Now carving was usually confined to the top rail and splat, although frames were sometimes reeded, and arms – when added – were scrolling in shape.

But classical decoration was not the only design source: some chairs were made in styles that had fallen from favor late in the previous century. One was chinoiserie, made popular by the future King George IV, in which chair frames were sometimes turned and decorated to resemble bamboo; the other was the Gothic style which incorporated elaborate carved motifs.

The Napoleonic wars meant that English designs were not so heavily influenced by the French trends that continued to dominate the rest of Europe. Designs were heavy and imposing, and most chairs were gilded or painted, or incorporated brass inlay. Swans, griffons, and other animals were used to decorate and even form the arms of chairs, which often had lion's legs and feet. Amphorae, horns of plenty, and military symbols such as fasces and wreaths were used on all types of furniture, including chairs.

REGENCY OPEN ARMCHAIR

Scrolling back and curved top rail. These are heavier looking than previously and typical of Regency chairs. On many such chairs, Britain's naval prowess was celebrated with the use of rope-twist carving and other nautical motifs.

Padded (originally caned) cross piece replaces the splat; splats were less common in the Regency.

Elbow chairs probably originated in France. On some such French chairs, the upholstery was removable so that it could be changed from summer to winter.

Anthemion-carved decoration on the chair leg is in keeping with the Egyptian influence.

Saber legs at the back taper outward.

Stylized decoration of this type, with animal forms used as supports, is rarely faked — pastiches are all too apparent.

The simulated bronze and parcel-gilt decoration imitates reeding. Chair frames are usually flush sided. Brass mounts may occasionally be later additions, particularly on continental pieces.

BLACK-PAINTED AND PARCEL-GILT CURULE
Also known as an X-frame chair, this design is adapted from the *sella curulis*, or stool used by the senators of ancient Rome. Although not robust, such chairs are fairly common.

Classical ornamentation derived from ancient Roman, Greek, and Egyptian motifs.

KLISMOS CHAIR
The reeded frame and bronzed and parcel-gilt decoration with applied rosettes on this Regency chair are a direct interpretation of the classical Greek original.

The lower back support is almost always decorated; here the turned rail is painted.

A drop-in seat replaces the original caned one. If the seat is removed, the holes for the caning should be clearly visible.

The seat rail is often decorated; here it is painted with light blue leaves.

REGENCY PAINTED SATINWOOD AND BEECH WINDOW SEAT
Furniture with painted decoration such as the flowers and floral trails on this seat was advocated by Thomas Sheraton in the 1803 supplement to his *Cabinet Directory*. Such a stool would have been placed in a window embrasure.

BALLOON-BACK CHAIRS

Perhaps the best-known 19th-century chair on both sides of the Atlantic, the balloon back developed from the dining chairs of the late Regency and William IV periods. The rectangular back typical of those periods was replaced by one that was "balloon" shaped, and both seat and legs were more sinuous in outline. Early examples were made with drop-in seats, but these were quickly superseded by stuffed seats. Balloon-back chairs were made in a variety of woods and finishes, and in papier mâché; they were also sometimes grained or painted, depending on whether they were intended for downstairs or upstairs rooms.

Hall chairs are somewhat similar in shape to balloon backs. Usually made in sets, sometimes with settees, they were designed to stand in the entrance hall of a house for use by waiting visitors. They were usually made of mahogany in the 18th century, but later oak became common. Since these chairs were mainly used by people wearing outdoor clothing, their seats were never upholstered. Most hall chairs have either carved decoration or are painted with their owner's coat-of-arms or monogram. Made from the 1730s until the late 19th century, they are found in many furniture design books.

SET OF 1840S ROSEWOOD BALLOON-BACK CHAIRS

Although balloon backs were usually made in sets of six, this is a set of four; this is not unknown since sets are often split up. Six chairs generally fetch proportionately more than four at sales and auctions, although four high-quality chairs such as these can be worth more than six of average quality.

These chairs are made of rosewood, but walnut and mahogany were also used for balloon backs.

The elaborately shaped and carved waisted backs are an indication of quality.

On cabriole-legged examples, the molding of the front seat rail frequently continues down the leg.

The D-shaped seats have a serpentine front rail, which is quite common on chairs intended for the drawing room, but less so on those used in the dining room or elsewhere.

These chairs are in the Louis XIV revival style: a similar piece is illustrated in a "Louis Quatorze" room illustrated in George Smith's Guide of 1828.

The cabriole legs end in a French foot. Such legs are quite delicate, making the chairs suitable only for occasional use. Always check whether they have been repaired — even a well-executed joint will not survive close inspection — and that they are original to the chair: in some cases, cabriole legs were used to replace less desirable turned ones.

The back legs are continuous with the back itself; a carved scroll marks the beginning of the leg.

The seats have been reupholstered in a sympathetic manner.

WILLIAM IV DINING CHAIR

This chair clearly shows the transition between Regency and balloon-back chairs. The carving is heavier in appearance than on Regency chairs, and the tapering, turned legs became a common feature of balloon backs intended for use in the dining room. The upholstered seat contains coiled springs.

HALL CHAIR

Dating from the mid-19th century, this mahogany hall chair with its pierced, star-shaped cartouche is an amalgam of styles among which French revival predominates. The overall shape of the back is similar to that of a balloon back, and it has the cabriole legs often found on balloon backs.

The dipped top rail of this chair, made in about 1840, is typical of early balloon backs. The rail is centered by a cartouche motif.

The heavier look of this back indicates that it dates from the 1860s and that it was probably used as a dining chair.

This is a typical drawing-room chair back. The pierced cresting and its elegant curves indicate that it is a product of the French revival style of the 1860s.

This back dates from the 1870s when balloon backs were going out of fashion. The arched back now has a splat — a feature not found on "true" balloon backs.

GOTHIC REVIVAL TO ARTS AND CRAFTS

hile early Regency chairs were generally restrained in overall style, with occasional whimsical or exuberant details, there was a marked change to more elaborate and overblown designs after 1815. Many were simply borrowings and reworkings of earlier styles. The balloon back reflected the "Louis revival" (with borrowings of elements from the reigns of Louis XIV, XV, and XVI); but the style was not universally admired, and a variety of revivals emerged as the century progressed. They include the Gothic revival, characterized by heavily carved dark oak furniture.

Gothic excesses, in their turn, were challenged by the reformed Gothic style which looked to simple architectural forms for inspiration; any carved decoration was not allowed to detract from the lines of the chair. By the 1870s the Aesthetic style was also popular. Heavily influenced by oriental styles, such chairs often had spindly, ebonized frames and incorporated Japanese stylistic elements.

At the same time, a series of "reformers" tried to fight against the eclecticism of mainstream design and what Charles Locke Eastlake described as the "intemperate use of curves." Perhaps the best-known exponent of reform is William Morris, the founder of the Arts and Crafts movement, who believed in simple designs that looked back to the craftsmanship of the Middle Ages. Morris's esthetic was echoed in Europe by the Art Nouveau and Wiener Werkstätte movements.

**MID-VICTORIAN
GOTHIC CHAIR**

The upholstery is inspired by a design by A.W.N. Pugin, one of the foremost exponents of the Gothic style. It may not be original, but the attribution adds to the esthetic appeal – rather than the value – of the chair.

Closely nailed brass studs are imitative of Elizabethan and Jacobean styling.

The design of the chair owes something to Pugin, although the castors have registry marks for 1877, 25 years after his death. Such castors are not an infallible guide to dating, since they are frequently added and removed, but when known to be original, as here, they add to the interest of a piece.

The corner blocks of seat frames are glued and screwed, with machine-made screws.

Crenelated top rail and foliate finials. During the 19th century, machine-cut dowels gradually replaced the traditional mortise and tenon joints as machinery was increasingly used in furniture manufacture.

Foliate spandrels, typical of the Gothic revival style.

Pierced trefoil band. On many chairs, machine carving, which has a much flatter appearance than hand carving, became the norm.

Carved Gothic arches are part of the chair's basic structure.

Cluster-column legs with quatrefoil heads. The use of the quatrefoil motif was not limited to Gothic-style chairs as Victorian furniture became more stylistically mixed.

GILTWOOD CORD STOOL

Similar in style to a piece by A.M.E. Fournier, this stool epitomizes the neorococo style of the Second Empire. The padded upholstered top reflects the 19th-century love of comfortable seating. The ornate twisted-rope stretchers, although broken, do not detract from the esthetic appeal of the piece.

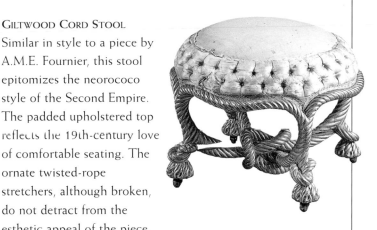

BENTWOOD CHILD'S CHAIR

This chair – stamped Thonet of Vienna – dates from about 1890. It is an example of the bentwood type of chair invented by the German Michael Thonet and first produced in the 1840s. Steam is used to bend the birch frame into shape, and the seat and back splats have the typical machine-stamped pattern. Made in their millions, these chairs are still common.

VICTORIAN CAST-IRON CHAIR

Cast iron became popular for use in inns, pubs, gardens, parks, and other locations where furniture was designed not to be moved. This Gothic-style chair was designed by Charles Green and made by the Masbro Stove Grate Company of Rotherham, England. The Victorian love of mixing styles is clearly in evidence: the cast roundel of a putto reading is in the Renaissance style of Luca della Robbia, while the bobbin turning is 17th century in origin.

ART NOUVEAU AND ART DECO STYLES

In the last quarter of the 19th century, designs were affected by the flowering of the Art Nouveau style which, although incorporating classical shapes, used natural forms for decoration. The style was popular throughout Europe; among its leading exponents were Gallé and Majorelle in France, Horta and van de Velde in Belgium, and Bugatti in Italy. It was less popular in Britain, where its advocates included Charles Rennie Mackintosh and C.F.A. Voysey. In Austria the Wiener Werkstätte, under the influence of Josef Hoffmann, was inspired by Mackintosh rather than following mainstream Art Nouveau ideas. Some followers of the style still used traditional chair-making techniques, others used machines.

The new style was not universally admired, and the manufacture of reproduction furniture continued. In addition to the enduring popularity of the Louis styles, Chippendale and Sheraton revivals flourished in England, where pieces can be distinguished from their period counterparts by their smaller proportions and the use of stringing as a decorative detail.

By the end of World War I, a style that had been emerging before the conflict began evolved fully. Known as Art Deco, it continued many of the trends of the Art Nouveau movement, but promoted the use of machinery instead of more traditional methods. And, instead of looking back to the mid-18th century for design inspiration, makers in the Deco style turned to the Louis XVI and Directoire periods, reinterpreted in a modernist manner.

STAINED OAK CHAIR

The best-known chairs by Charles Rennie Mackintosh have high backs which are in fact prone to damage. This low-backed example is much sturdier.

This chair was designed for Glasgow's Argyle Street Tea Rooms by Mackintosh, an architect who, like Robert Adam, designed every feature of his interiors, including the furniture.

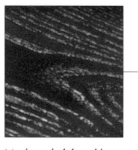

Mackintosh did not like to leave wood in an untreated state, but preferred to use stained or painted finishes, often white or, as here, flat black.

The side panels are set at right angles to the seat and extend below it.

The dimensions of Mackintosh's chairs of the same design often vary as, although he used professional cabinetmakers, he visited the workshops often, giving advice and direction.

The turned legs extend form the arm supports at the front and the back uprights at the back.

A typical feature of Mackintosh chairs is the concentrated use of vertical lines; this is demonstrated here in the finials on each side of the splat.

OAK OPEN CHAIR

This rush-seated chair, designed by M.H. Baillie-Scott, is similar to those made by Gustave Stickley in America, where the values of the Arts and Crafts movement were gaining a foothold. Although Arts and Crafts furniture was based on traditional country designs and techniques, pieces are often more sophisticated in execution than this chair, which shows the simplicity favored by Baillie-Scott.

ARTS AND CRAFTS CHAIR

With its narrow, tapering back and arrow-shaped splat, this chair combines the typical style of Arts and Crafts with the emerging so-called Quaint style – England's attempt at interpreting Art Nouveau.

BUGATTI ROCKING CHAIR

Bugatti is perhaps best known for his furniture incorporating Moorish design elements. This beech rocking chair, however, is much simpler in influence, with the open oval side panels deriving from Romanesque architecture. The use of parchment is typical of Bugatti's work.

Mackintosh's love of gentle curves is apparent in this chair.

Mackintosh's low-backed chairs are reproduced less frequently than his high-backed designs. Reproductions are obvious from the construction methods used: genuine Mackintosh chairs are hand crafted.

MACASSAR EBONY ARMCHAIR

The influence of the Directoire period can be seen in this chair, one of a set of six attributed to Paul Kiss. The use of macassar ebony combined with brown hide upholstery and the hammered brass borders and top rail, however, are pure Art Deco elements. Kiss is best known for his wrought-iron furniture; here the legs end in copper feet.

UPHOLSTERED FURNITURE

It is difficult to imagine today, when fully upholstered furniture is so familiar, that before upholstery started to become more common in the houses of the rich in the 18th century, loose cushions were the only means of providing a little comfort when sitting on a wooden chair or settee.

Although many chairs have lost their original coverings, enough survive in both good and poor condition to give an accurate picture of how they looked new. Velvets, silks, damasks, and needlework were all used in the 18th century to cover chairs and sofas. Their patterns were often elaborate, as the silks made in Lyons in France and Spitalfields in London testify. Chintzes, which remain popular, were introduced toward the end of the 18th century.

The widespread increase in the popularity of upholstered furniture since the mid-19th century has resulted in a corresponding increase in the choice of fabrics available, at all price levels. As a result, it is possible to obtain suitable fabrics to reupholster period furniture, although this can be a costly process.

BOLSTER
A long narrow cylindrical-shaped cushion.

PADDED BACK
The down-scrolling shape of this back is typical of Regency chaises longues. It ends in a scroll terminal.

GRECIAN LEG
A type of saber leg popular on Regency seating furniture. On chairs most saber legs curve to the front; on sofas they curve to the side.

FRAME
The basic structural components of a chair or settee onto which webbing, stuffing, and upholstery are nailed.

OTHER USEFUL TERMS

A CHASSIS Used to describe a style of upholstery found on some 18th-century French chairs, by which the back, seat, and arm rests were removable so that the upholstery could be changed, usually from summer to winter.

LUGS Another term for the wings of a wing chair.

SERPENTINE FRONT Sinuous double-curved front found on chair seats, particularly popular in the 18th century.

WEBBING The narrow bands of strong material, such as jute, which are interwoven and secured across the base of the seat rails on a chair or settee to support the stuffed or sprung upholstery.

ELBOW PAD
The upholstered section of an arm on which the sitter's arm rests.

SEAT RAIL
The horizontal rail which forms the seat of a chair.

SHOW WOOD
The visible wood on an upholstered piece of furniture.

SCROLL END
The lower arm at one end of some sofas and daybeds. It may scroll inward or outward. Some chairs and sofas have scrolling outward-turning cylinder-shaped arms, known as scroll arms.

WING
A side projection at head level found on chairs from the 18th century onward, designed to protect the sitter from drafts.

SQUAB
A loose cushion.

GIMP
Woven braided ribbon-type fabric used to cover the upholstery nails on chairs or settees.

CASTOR WITH BRASS CAP
Brass caps were often an integral part of the castor; in the Regency lion's paw caps were also popular.

STRETCHER
The horizontal strut or rail between the legs of a chair or table.

FABRICS AND FINISHES

The fragility of some fabrics and changing styles and tastes over the years, has meant that many upholstered pieces of furniture no longer have their original upholstery – some may well have been reupholstered more than once. If this is the case, there will be tack marks where the material was attached to the frame.

Trimmings were an important feature of upholstered chairs, and they, too, varied in style from period to period. This needs to be considered when reupholstering chairs and sofas since a piece reupholstered without attention to all details can be jarring and aesthetically unappealing.

Seat types can be a useful guide to dating: drop-in seats first appeared in the late 17th century and coiled springs in the 1820s; stylistic devices on the frame are also helpful clues.

Fringe

Fringes were particularly popular as a decorative edging in the 17th and 19th centuries, generally less so in the 18th, although the fringe above is from an Italian 18th-century chair

From the mid-17th century, fringe designs became more elaborate, the fringe above is from a George III chair.

Gimp

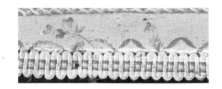

Braid or gimp is used to cover the upholstery nails on chairs or settees. The braid above is from an Austrian settee.

Gimp from a Louis XV armchair made by Jean Baptiste Tilliard.

Textiles

If antique furniture is to be used, it is often necessary to re-cover a piece. When to reupholster tends to be a matter of personal choice: one person may be happy to live with original upholstery, whatever its condition, for as long as possible, another may not. For an important piece of furniture, it is advisable to seek conservation advice, although this may limit usability. It is important always to choose a suitable period-style fabric when reupholstering.

Damask cover for a stool 16th century

Velvet upholstery with gold and silver thread 17th century

Fabric designed by E.W. Godwin (1833–86) for a chair

Brocaded silk brocatelle, woven by Lemire père et fils, Lyons 1850

Gros and petit point needlework seat cover mid-18th century

Nails and trimming

Leather is probably the oldest "fabric" for covering seating furniture, although most early leather upholstery has not survived in good condition. It can also, as on this George III open armchair, be used to cover buttons and decorative upholstery nails.

On fabric-covered chairs, gimp or nails may used to cover the upholstery nails and as decorative features in their own right. On this mid-Georgian Irish walnut chair, closely spaced brass nails have been used along the seat rail, wing edges and arm rests.

Chintz, printed, patterned cotton
with a glazed finish
1770

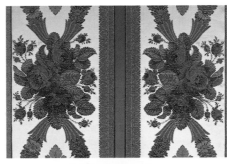

Satin by Cousin and Berny
Bissardon, Lyons
1811

French embroidered velvet
by the Grand brothers
1811

"Daffodil" chintz designed
by William Morris
1875

Damask by Berard
and Ferrand, Lyons
1889

"The Cortège of Orpheus" silk damask
designed by Raoul Dufy and woven by
Bianchini-Ferier 1921

SETTEES AND SOFAS

The terms settee and sofa have been used since the early 18th century. Although today considered interchangeable – both describe an upholstered seat with a back and arms which is large enough for at least two people to sit comfortably – there is a slight difference between the two. Strictly speaking, the term sofa applies to larger pieces on which a person could recline. Both sofas and settees were usually made as part of a set of seating furniture.

They evolved from the wooden settles of the Middle Ages, and by the first half of the 17th century settees of a design similar to the back stool were being made. After the Restoration in 1660, the demand in Britain for furniture based on continental styles prompted the development of settees that resembled upholstered wing chairs of the William and Mary period. One style that remained popular throughout the 18th century was the chair-back settee which, as

the name suggests, consisted of two or more wooden chair backs joined together, with a single upholstered seat.

In the 19th century, sofas, like most other forms of furniture, were being made in a variety of styles, including rococo revival and Gothic revival. The chesterfield, which originally appeared in about 1880, was the first fully upholstered settee and put spring upholstery to good use. No one knows for sure whether its

VICTORIAN CHESTERFIELD

Back and scrolled arms are the same height. This design has remained largely unchanged for more than a century.

Deep-buttoned leather upholstery is now more usual, but this was not originally the case and normally indicates that the sofa has been reupholstered. The seat should be tight fitting, without separate cushions.

Short turned legs are common, and many chesterfields also have castors. Expect the feet and underframe to show signs of wear.

Coiled steel springs, sitting on a webbing base and tied to the frame, were introduced in the first half of the 19th century. A sprung seat has more "give" than one that is simply padded and is therefore more comfortable.

name derives from the Derbyshire town
or from one of the earls of Chesterfield.

One variant of the sofa is the daybed, a
long upholstered seat on legs, with a fixed
or adjustable head, and sometimes foot,
and usually inclined to allow the user to lie
in comfort. Daybeds have been used since
the 17th century. Perhaps the best-known
daybed is the Regency chaise longue,
which has one or two scrolled ends and
an upholstered, often down-curving, back.

*Acanthus
carving on the
mahogany
frame is an
unusual but
pleasing touch.*

GEORGE II SETTEE
This is one of a pair of richly carved mahogany settees made
in the 1750s, and the serpentine back and outscrolled arms are
typical of the period. The backs of some French sofas made at
this time were carved to fit the design of a room's paneling.

GEORGE I TRIPLE CHAIR-BACK SETTEE
This walnut settee has the typical decorative details, such
as shells, lion masks, and ball and claw feet, of chairs
of the period. The needlework drop-in seat
cover is contemporary. Stuffed seats
can also be found on these settees.

WALNUT NEOCLASSICAL DAYBED
Ribbon twists, tied flower heads, laurel
leaves, and berries adorn the heavily carved
frame of this daybed. The outward-tapering legs are also carved
with leaves and foliage. The back, seat, and long separate cushion
are padded for extra comfort and upholstered in silk. Its length
of more than 6 feet (1.8 m) allows the sitter to recline in comfort.

UPHOLSTERED CHAIRS

Loose cushions were used to offer the sitter a measure of comfort on 16th-century oak chairs, but it was not until the beginning of the 17th century that fully upholstered chairs developed. Sets of upholstered seating furniture have been made for houses since then, and although there are very few early sets in existence, many fine examples have survived from the late 17th century onward.

High-backed upholstered chairs with wings and an adjustable back were made in the second half of the 17th century. Known as sleeping chairs, they were the precursors of the fixed-back, fully upholstered wing chairs which had emerged by the end of the century. Wing, or easy, chairs remained fashionable throughout the 18th century. In 18th-century France, one of the most popular chairs was the bergère in which, in addition to the back and seat, the sides were also upholstered. Most bergères do not have wings.

In 1828 the coiled spring was introduced, making chairs much more comfortable. Rapid population growth in the first half of the 19th century, in both the United States and Europe, meant that by 1850 there was a huge demand for upholstered furniture by all classes of society and not, as before, simply by the rich. This trend has continued into the 20th century.

GEORGE II WALNUT WING ARMCHAIR

The rectangular back flows into the wings; before about 1730 there was a stronger division between the back and wings. Eventually both back and wings were of the same height.

Wings developed to help protect the sitter from drafts. They have often been repaired.

Outward-scrolling arms. Later examples may have outswept down-scrolling arms.

Contemporary gros- and petit-point polychrome needlework. The original fabric always adds to the value of an upholstered chair. Chairs of this period were also upholstered in velvet, but needlework is more desirable. Many chair frames show tack holes where they have been reupholstered over the years.

A deep apron was common before the introduction of springs in the 19th century. A squab cushion on top adds to the sitter's comfort.

Square back legs which taper outward slightly. Legs are often replaced: check that wood, shape, and carving are appropriate.

Decorative rivets, braid or
gimp may be found along
the edge of the wing.

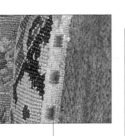

GEORGE II LIBRARY OPEN ARMCHAIR
This grained and parcel-gilt chair is an
English version of the French
bergère and was originally part
of a set of eight armchairs and
a settee. The square
back is typical of
upholstered chairs
of the period. The
plump cushion is
down-filled.

Check the height of
a wing armchair.
early examples are
proportionately taller
than later models.

Back view

Front view

Original or early
replacement leather and
fabric upholstery will
show wear on the ends
of the arms.

RUSSIAN ORMOLU-MOUNTED BERGÈRE
This early 19th-century mahogany bergère is a fine later
example of the Russian neoclassical style. It is decorated
with ormolu mounts drawn from classical sources. Similar
types of mounts are also found on Empire chairs.

VICTORIAN SPOONBACK CHAIR
Made without arms to allow for the
voluminous dresses of the day, these
chairs are sometimes called ladies'
chairs. Buttonback upholstery was
popular in the Victorian era
because of the way it "fitted" the
sitter's contours. Original
fabric upholstery is
usually not in
good condition;
contemporary
leather upholstery
is not common
on such chairs.

Cabriole legs ending in pad feet. Any
carving on the knee should stand out
from the leg. Until the late 18th century,
legs were often joined by stretchers.

TABLES

One of the most important features of daily life, tables have been part of the human experience for centuries. Every home, from grandest palace to humblest cottage, has at least one table around which family and friends gather for convivial meals and conversation. Styles of table vary from country to country, and woods wax and wane in popularity, but common themes are evident in their design: trestle tables, for example, are found throughout Europe and America.

Variations on the design of dining tables are endless, but so too are the different types of tables themselves. Some were made simply to be ornamental, to stand against a wall and complement a design scheme. Others were made for occasional use, such as when tea was served. This is seen in M.B. Olivier's 18th-century painting, *Le thé à l'anglaise*, in which the Prince of Conti's household takes tea from a range of tables, while the young Mozart plays to the company. Still more were functional – a support for candles or candelabra, for example, or a surface on which to play cards. Finally, there were those tables that, for reasons of space or economy or design innovation, served many purposes: a support for a meal, a surface on which to lay a book or write a letter, and an ornamental piece of furniture.

PARQUETRY
Veneers laid in a geometric pattern, used for decorative effect.

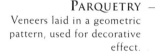

OTHER USEFUL TERMS

BIRDCAGE MECHANISM Hinged columnar device which allows a table top to be tilted.

COLUMN Circular vertical post which can be used as a support or a decorative feature.

CONCERTINA MECHANISM The means by which the back legs of a card table can be pulled out to extend a hinged frieze rail that supports the flap top when opened.

CUT-CARD WORK Fret-cut lattice glued to the face of a piece of furniture to simulate carving.

FLY BRACKET The hinged piece of wood that supports a table flap when open, found on Pembroke and other folding tables.

GALLERY RAIL The raised border of a table, desk, or tray, often made of miniature wooden or metal spindles or fretwork.

LOPER The pull-out wooden rails that support the leaf of a table.

PEGGED TABLE An early piece that could be dismantled for ease of movement.

UNDERTIER A shaped shelf found between a table's legs, some way beneath the top.

PEDESTAL
The central column, often shaped, that supports a table. Larger tables may be supported by more than one pedestal.

PLATFORM
The shaped base, supported by short legs or feet, from which the pedestal rises on some tables.

RULE JOINT
Joint found on gate-leg tables and screens whereby the two adjoining surfaces are shaped to leave no gap when the object is open.

TOP
Table tops are often elaborately decorated with marquetry, parquetry, matched veneers, or inlay. Some small tables have plain tops and decorated legs or pedestals – this indicates that the top was covered with a cloth when in use.

CROSSBANDING
Decorative effect created by inserting a piece of wood cut across the grain into another cut with the grain.

GATE-LEG
A hinged leg which can be opened outward to support a table flap.

STRETCHER
The horizontal strut or rail found between the legs of tables or chairs; here it is ball turned.

LEAF
Any extra piece of wood that may be inserted, pulled out, or lifted up to extend a table.

BRASS HINGE
Hinges are usually made of brass; they often break which can cause damage to the table top, the leaf, or both.

APRON
The shaped wooden edging beneath the top of a table or seat rail of a chair; also found below the drawer line of case furniture.

CARVING
A design in wood worked for decorative effect. Carving is sometimes done as an integral part of the piece, and sometimes worked separately and glued or tenoned in place.

WOODEN HANDLE
The handles of sofa tables are usually made of brass or wood; they are often replaced.

FRIEZE DRAWER
A drawer in the frieze or framework just below a table top.

SCROLL FOOT
A foot that curves outward and back on itself. Here it is decorated with classical motifs.

CASTOR
A small wheel, made of wood, china, brass, or leather, attached to the bottom of the feet of tables or chairs, allowing them to be moved without having to be lifted.

DESIGN DETAILS

Table legs and feet can help in identifying when a table was made. There are so many different types of tables, however, that features common to a particular type can also play a part. Three types of folding mechanisms are found on card tables, for example, and the use of one or the other can be a guide to dating, as well as a measure of the table's quality. Similarly, the diameter of gate-leg tables as well as the patented mechanisms of some 19th-century dining tables can indicate when the table was made.

Basic shapes and decorative details have changed over the years, a factor which may help in determining whether a piece is period or not. Many later tables had decoration common to a former period added to make them more desirable.

Banding and stringing

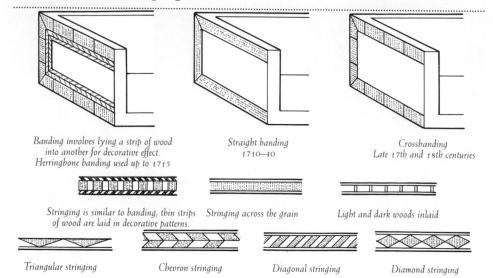

Banding involves lying a strip of wood into another for decorative effect. Herringbone banding used up to 1715

Straight banding 1710–40

Crossbanding Late 17th and 18th centuries

Stringing is similar to banding; thin strips of wood are laid in decorative patterns.

Stringing across the grain

Light and dark woods inlaid

Triangular stringing

Chevron stringing

Diagonal stringing

Diamond stringing

Folding and extending mechanisms

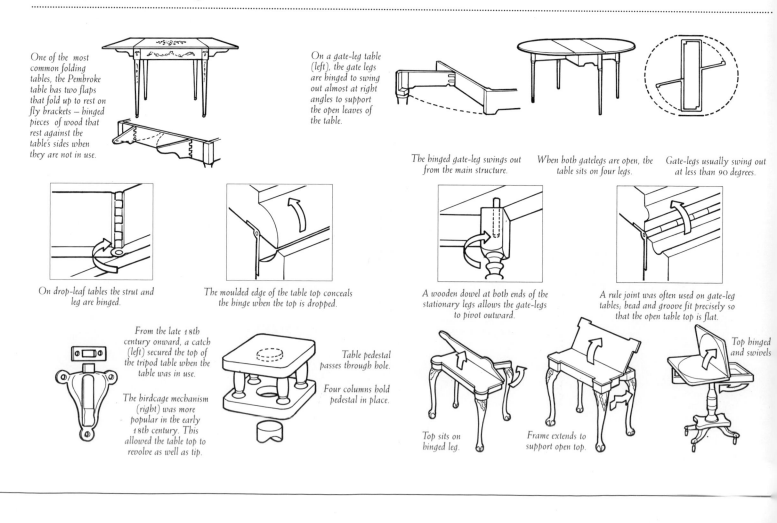

One of the most common folding tables, the Pembroke table has two flaps that fold up to rest on fly brackets – hinged pieces of wood that rest against the table's sides when they are not in use.

On a gate-leg table (left), the gate legs are hinged to swing out almost at right angles to support the open leaves of the table.

The hinged gate-leg swings out from the main structure.

When both gatelegs are open, the table sits on four legs.

Gate-legs usually swing out at less than 90 degrees.

On drop-leaf tables the strut and leg are hinged.

The moulded edge of the table top conceals the hinge when the top is dropped.

A wooden dowel at both ends of the stationary legs allows the gate-legs to pivot outward.

A rule joint was often used on gate-leg tables, bead and groove fit precisely so that the open table top is flat.

From the late 18th century onward, a catch (left) secured the top of the tripod table when the table was in use.

The birdcage mechanism (right) was more popular in the early 18th century. This allowed the table top to revolve as well as tip.

Table pedestal passes through hole.

Four columns hold pedestal in place.

Top sits on hinged leg.

Frame extends to support open top.

Top hinged and swivels

Legs for tripod tables

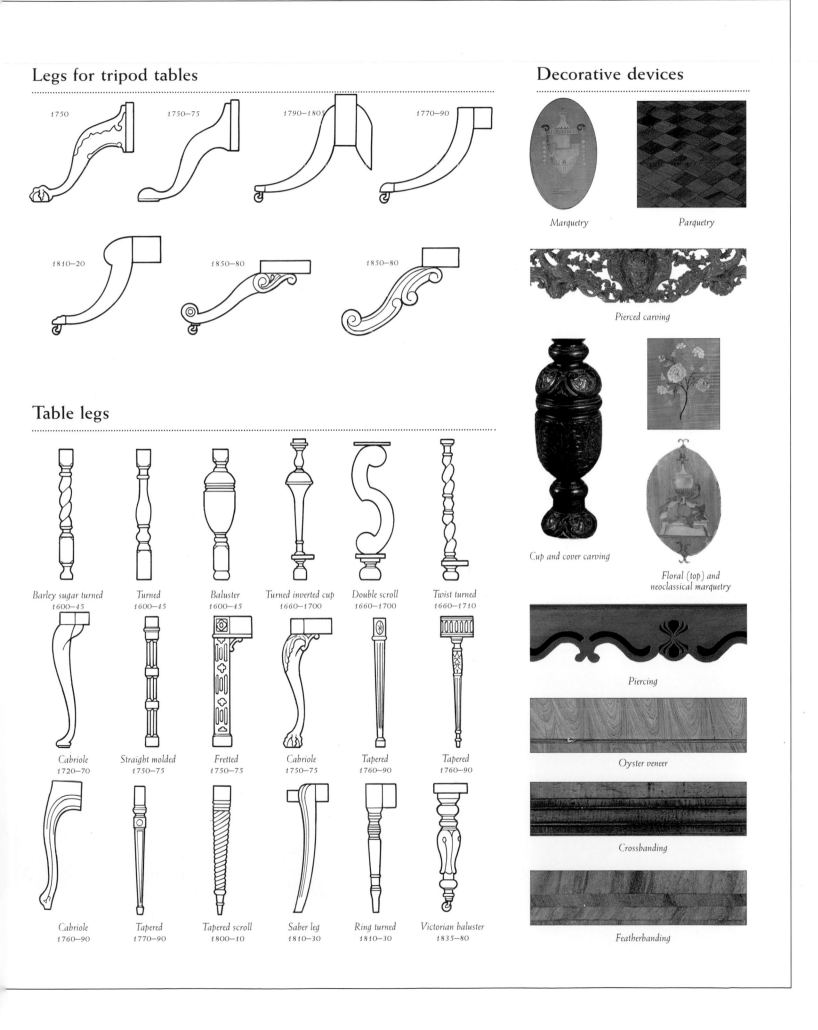

1750

1750–75

1790–1805

1770–90

1810–20

1850–80

1850–80

Table legs

Barley sugar turned
1600–45

Turned
1600–45

Baluster
1600–45

Turned inverted cup
1660–1700

Double scroll
1660–1700

Twist turned
1660–1710

Cabriole
1720–70

Straight molded
1750–75

Fretted
1750–75

Cabriole
1750–75

Tapered
1760–90

Tapered
1760–90

Cabriole
1760–90

Tapered
1770–90

Tapered scroll
1800–10

Saber leg
1810–30

Ring turned
1810–30

Victorian baluster
1835–80

Decorative devices

Marquetry

Parquetry

Pierced carving

Cup and cover carving

*Floral (top) and
neoclassical marquetry*

Piercing

Oyster veneer

Crossbanding

Featherbanding

EARLY DINING TABLES

The earliest surviving type of dining table is the trestle table used in the Middle Ages. Since the top was made from long wooden planks resting on trestles, such tables could be dismantled and moved to the side of the hall when space was needed for other activities. In medieval times, the assembled company ate together in the great hall, with the master and mistress of the house usually seated at a smaller table raised on a dais. By the mid-16th century, however, it had become more common for the master and his family to eat in a separate room, and more permanent tables evolved. The term refectory table has been applied to these early "solid" tables since the 19th century. Styles varied, but such tables were popular all over Europe.

In the mid-17th century gate-leg tables, which had flaps that could be folded down when the table was not in use, became popular for dining. Initially, these tables were often quite large – up to 8 feet (2.4 m) in diameter – but as time went by and it became fashionable to use several small tables rather than one large one, they became smaller.

EARLY 17TH-CENTURY OAK DRAW-LEAF REFECTORY TABLE

The rectangular top of most refectory tables consists of two or three planks and should always have the good patina that comes with age and use. Check that it is not a later copy made from old floorboards – there should be signs of filled-in holes if it is.

The underside of a table's top edge should show signs of handling resulting from years of use.

The turned legs have a bulbous center section carved with scrolls and foliage. This shape was popular in the Elizabethan era and is known as cup and cover decoration.

The table is made entirely from oak, with no other woods used in its construction.

Dowels should stand out from the surface, due to shrinkage over the centuries.

The motif of interlaced arches carved on the frieze is typical of the period and is repeated evenly between the legs. If this is not the case, the table may have been shortened at some stage, or been put together with pieces of wood from different sources.

Oak was the most popular furniture wood in Britain in the 17th century.

Brackets pull out to hold open leaves.

The leaves, which rest on a bed under the table top when not in use, are later replacements. This is not uncommon. This style of table was much copied in the 19th and early 20th centuries, and reproductions are still made: these can be identified from the method of construction.

The feet are carved in one piece with the legs; the stretchers are then doweled to them.

Stretchers and legs show the expected uneven signs of wear; edges have been rounded and are no longer as sharp as when the table was first made.

SPANISH WALNUT DINING TABLE
Made in the late 17th century, this table is a traditional style that dates back at least a century earlier. The plank top, which should always have a square edge as here, is supported on ring-turned splay supports and scrolled iron stretchers.

TUSCAN WALNUT REFECTORY TABLE
This table is typical of those made in Italy in the 16th century and is some 11½ feet (3.5 m) long. The pedestal-shaped supports reflect the contemporary interest in architectural motifs. Some tables of this period have end supports modeled on the sarcophagi of ancient Rome.

CHARLES II YEW GATE-LEG DINING TABLE
The plain edge of the oval twin-flap top is correct for this period. The bobbin-turned stretchers and the barley-twist and square legs are of the right thickness; they always look too thin on copies.

EXTENDING DINING TABLES

The custom of having several small, rather than one large, table in the dining room continued into the 18th century, but the formerly popular gate-leg table was soon superseded by an improved version that no longer had "gates" or stretchers between the legs. Known as a drop-leaf table, this type had four legs, two of which swung out on a knuckle hinge to support the flaps; early examples had cabriole legs often ending in pad feet, but by the middle of the century, such tables more often stood on straight legs.

In the second half of the century, practices changed, and it became more usual to sit at one large table. Of these, one type had free-standing D-shaped end sections on tapering legs and a central gate-leg section which could be used with the flaps either up or down to provide extra seating space. But as before, the drawback was the number of legs, which tended to get in the diners' way.

This problem was solved in the 1780s with the introduction of the pedestal dining table. Like previous styles, it could be equipped with extra leaves to extend its length.

Breakfast tables are a smaller variation of the pedestal table, made for more intimate family meals. They often have tilt-tops so that they can be kept in a corner of the room when not in use. Pedestal tables of all sizes have been reproduced, and "married" examples are not uncommon.

REGENCY MAHOGANY EXTENDING DINING TABLE

The top is D-shaped. Any decoration on the top should match that on the legs. Such tables have often been split up into their components in the past and then married with different parts at a later date.

Pedestal tables made in the 18th century do not have a frieze or apron.

The four pedestals supporting each end of the top are turned.

Brass caps and castors are correct for the period; lion's paw castors were also common at this time.

The concave-sided platforms between the pedestals are not original, although such platforms are a common feature of this type of table.

The three additional leaves here are later replacements. Color is one indicator, although leaves are often darker than the rest of the table since they have not been exposed to the light as often.

The table edge is molded; molding on the table itself and on the leaves should match.

The downswept legs have the typical "knees" of Regency period tables.

Molding on the downswept legs matches that on the top.

Molded roundels decorate the tops of the legs.

CLASSICAL CARVED MAHOGANY BREAKFAST TABLE

Attributed to Duncan Phyfe, this table has a clover-shaped drop-leaf at each end. The frieze drawer is flanked by carved waterleaf panels, a motif found on the base of the baluster supports and the knees. The sides of the base, with its central pineapple, are carved with leaves and fluted. The hairy paw feet end in castors.

GEORGE III MAHOGANY DINING TABLE

This type of table was popular in both the United States and England. The two D-shaped ends could be used as freestanding side tables or combined to form an oval table; the middle section could be used alone as a rectangular gate-leg table. The inconvenience to sitters of the supporting legs is quite apparent.

GEORGE III MAHOGANY TWIN-PEDESTAL DINING TABLE

The central section of this table is a drop-leaf, with folding supports similar to the tripod pedestals supporting each end section. This so-called Cumberland action — by which the leaves are supported without affecting the sitters — was named after the Duke of Cumberland, George III's brother and reputed first owner of such a table.

CENTER AND DINING TABLES

In the 19th century, circular pedestal tables, often more than 4 feet (1.2 m) in diameter, stood in the center of the drawing room, to be used for both dining and playing the card game lanterloo, hence the name loo tables by which they are also known. Early in the century, rosewood and mahogany were the preferred woods, but later, burl-walnut veneers, often inlaid with brass, marquetry, mother-of-pearl, or exotic woods, grew in popularity. As machine carving became more common, columns and legs were often heavily carved, to complement table tops that were also becoming ever more elaborate.

Although large dining tables continued to be made in a variety of styles in the 19th century, mechanical tables were in great demand. From about 1800 onward, various designs appeared, which had in common some sort of mechanical action to extend either circular or rectangular tables so that extra leaves could be inserted. The leaves rested on bearers under the table, thereby eliminating the need for extra legs.

To reflect their success, the wealthy middle classes sought opulent furniture, much of it in one of the many revival styles that dominated the 19th century, and a great deal of heavily carved Gothic-style furniture was made. But as the century progressed, an increasing number of "reformers," including A.W.N. Pugin, Charles Eastlake, and William Morris and other adherents of the Arts and Crafts movement, began to advocate a return to simple methods of construction and a restraint in using unnecessary ornament or decoration. Their influence was eventually felt even in mainstream furniture production.

It is worth remembering that Victorian tables are being copied today, using thin machine-cut veneers or marquetry.

LOUIS XVIII BURL-ELM AND MARQUETRY CENTER TABLE

A printed label inscribed CHÂTEAU DES TUILERIES 1829 with, written on it, the inventory number 1047 and SALON DE FAMILLE DU ROI is attached to this table. It was made by Louis-François-Laurent Puteaux and was in fact first recorded at the Tuileries in 1816.

Ormolu figures of Victory flanked by arrows are mounted on the pentagonal support. Brass hardware used on modern copies is of inferior quality to that used on period tables.

The top of this table does not tilt.

Concave sides are typical of the plinths of 19th-century pedestal tables. Three-sided concave plinths are common on small Regency tables.

Ormolu wreaths decorate the edges of the plinth.

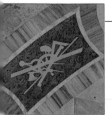

Panels representing Science, Painting, Gardening, Architecture, Music, and Navigation.

EARLY VICTORIAN OAK DINING TABLE
Typical of the Gothic revival style popular in many countries during the 19th century, this table's foliate-carved frieze looks too fussy with the pierced Gothic tracery.

BIEDERMEIER FOLDING BREAKFAST TABLE
A style that originated in Germany and Austria, Biedermeier was simpler and more classically elegant than Empire furniture. Architectural forms were popular, and light-colored fruitwoods were frequently used. The style influenced designs in Eastern Europe, including Russia, and in Scandinavia.

The table top is beautifully inlaid with geometrically interlaced petals of mahogany and maple which radiate outward from a central rosette toward the tulipwood crossbanding and border, which is set with emblem and wreath inlaid panels.

The central rosette and mother-of-pearl wreath are not original but replace an ivory plaque engraved with a portrait of Henri IV within the cypher of Louis XVIII. This alteration was carried out prior to the table's sale in 1831 as "surplus to requirements."

Pentagonal plinth on turned feet. Remember that dirt and dust accumulate unevenly over the years; if the coating is too even, it could have been applied later, so be wary of its authenticity.

MAHOGANY, EBONY, AND MARQUETRY CENTER TABLE
Marquetry decoration, as here, can be found on many pedestal tables. Replacing a damaged leather table top can be costly, but when the table is otherwise in good condition it is worth doing.

FOLDING TABLES

In the 18th century, it was customary to move furniture around a room to suit the needs of the occupants, a practice that resulted in the need for a number of "occasional" tables. Many of these tables were either originally fitted with castors or have had them added. The earliest castors, made in the late 17th century, were wooden and rigid so that, until the introduction of the axle pin, it was possible to push furniture only backward or forward. By the mid-18th century, leather castors were being used, but they were soon superseded by brass. Square-toe or cup shapes were used in the late 18th century, but many Regency designers favored the lion's paw, among others; in the Victorian period, ceramic castors were also used.

The Pembroke table is typical of these movable, folding tables, and could be used for needlework, drawing, writing, and meals. Pembroke tables are usually rectangular or oval, with a drawer in the central section and a hinged drop-leaf at each side. An early example – called a breakfast table – can be found in Chippendale's designs.

In the late 18th century, a type of table defined by Sheraton in 1803 as "used before a sofa" to allow the lady of the house to draw, write, or read evolved from the Pembroke table. Sofa tables, particularly popular in the Regency period, are rectangular with a drop-leaf at each end and – usually – two drawers in the frieze. Some have brass or ebony inlay. Early sofa tables have supports at each end, but from about 1812 they were also made with a central pedestal support. Both sofa and Pembroke tables were popular in the United States as well as Britain.

In the 19th century, Sutherland tables became popular. These were drop-flap gate-leg tables which when extended might measure 40 inches (1 m) or more, but only a quarter of that when they were closed.

GEORGE III SATINWOOD MARQUETRY, PAINTED, AND PARCEL-GILT PEMBROKE TABLE

Marquetry or painted decoration was added to many plain Pembroke tables made in the 18th century to "improve" them. Pembroke tables have also been much copied.

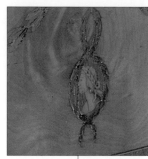

The serpentine-shaped marquetry top of this table is possibly by Thomas Chippendale: it is very similar to a pair of card tables thought to have been supplied by him at Newby Hall, Yorkshire, England.

Carving of ribbon-tied flowers.

This drawer is a later addition, but most Pembroke tables have a frieze drawer at one end and a false drawer front at the other. The drawer outline should echo the shape of the top.

The white-painted and parcel-gilt legs may not have originally "belonged" with the top.

The individual components of the marquetry top work as well when the flaps are down as when they are open.

The marquetry decoration is neoclassically inspired. The central ammonite flower and conch shell medallion, scrolling acanthus, and the swags of husks with their medallions of Apollo come together as an overall design when the flaps are up.

The side flaps, when extended, are supported by fly brackets, narrow pieces of wood that are hinged so that they can be folded outward to act as supports.

The cabriole legs are unusual; it is more common for Pembroke tables to have square tapering legs.

Brass castors may have been subject to a lot of wear since these tables were more useful if they could be moved around. Expect castors to have been replaced – but check that the replacements are in a sympathetic style.

REGENCY BURL-ELM SOFA TABLE

Attributed to George Bullock, this table without drop-flaps has a turned stretcher between the two end supports – a feature often found on sofa tables. Sofa tables were made in Europe as well as Britain; this holly inlay is inspired by French designs.

GEORGE III MAHOGANY PEMBROKE TABLE

This Gothic-style table is supported on eight cluster-column legs (four stationary and four that swing out to support the open leaves) and is a variation of the spider-leg table first seen in the 18th century. It can be regarded as a precursor of the 19th-century Sutherland table.

REGENCY ROSEWOOD CROSSBANDED AND BRASS-MOUNTED SOFA TABLE

This classic example of the type of sofa table with end supports is fitted with two drawers on one side and drawer fronts on the other, a common practice on such tables. It has brass cappings and castors.

SIDE TABLES

Intended to stand against a wall, side tables have been used since the late 15th century. From the 17th century, they played an increasingly important role in house furnishing, either as practical tables or as part of a great interior design scheme.

One traditional type is rectangular, with an overhanging top and frieze drawer, and is supported by four legs. Styling reflects the period in which these tables were made, and they were used for many purposes – as writing tables in the library, dressing tables in the bedroom, serving tables in the dining room, and for displaying ornaments.

In the more affluent houses of the 18th and 19th centuries, two forms of side table predominated. The first was the console table, which originated in France. This is a table attached to the wall at the back and supported by legs at the front. The second was the pier table, designed to stand in the space between two windows (known as a pier). Usually highly decorated, these tables were often made in pairs and formed an integral part of a room's design scheme; a mirror often hung above them to reflect both the top and the light from a candelabrum placed there. Some English console tables have intertwined dolphins or eagles with outspread wings as supports.

GEORGE III SATINWOOD SIDE TABLE

Parcel-gilt urn on white-painted background.

Corners are vulnerable to knocks, and veneers are by their nature fragile, but sympathetic restoration need not affect value.

Carved with anthemia, the frieze is typical of the designs of Robert Adam and reflects the influence of architectural motifs in decoration of the period.

The tapering legs of this table demonstrate that furniture was becoming much lighter in appearance when compared to the heavier lines used earlier in the century.

Parcel gildin Regilding is common sinc fragile legs a easily knock Copies made the 19th century are usually gild

Legs and feet are typical of the period.

The tops of the legs are carved with lotus leaves and acanthus, typical neoclassical motifs.

The backs of side tables are always
roughly finished as they were
designed to stand against the wall.

The marquetry urn is a
particularly fine piece of
neoclassical decoration.

rolling foliate inlay
and tulipwood
crossbanding.

The neoclassical marquetry
decoration of this pier table's
top would have been reflected
by the mirror behind it and lit
at night by a candelabrum
standing on it.

Pier tables must be
supported at the back.

REGENCY WALNUT SIDE TABLE

Marble tops need sturdy frames to support them, but this finely
carved example shows how the carver's skill could make them
seem light and delicate. Gilding or painted decoration is usually
found only on pine frames.

COLONIAL ROSEWOOD SIDE TABLE

This early 18th-century table of Dutch or Portuguese colonial
origin is a good example of the traditional type of side table
popular in the 17th and 18th centuries. The central fifth leg is
unusual on this type of table.

EMPIRE MAHOGANY SIDE TABLE

Dating from the early 19th century, this table is of a shape and
style that was also popular in England. Some examples have a
mirror plate between the back legs to increase the reflected light.
A missing mirror should be obvious from screw holes in the back.

CARD AND GAME TABLES

The first specialist game tables date from the late 17th century. They had a folding top which was supported by two gate legs when opened, but this was uncomfortable for the players as the stretchers and legs got in their way.

The situation improved during Queen Anne's reign with the introduction of the cabriole leg. Tables were now fitted with a hinged back leg that could be swung out to support the unfolded top; the design was later modified so that both back legs were hinged for use as supports. The more expensive card tables were fitted with an accordion-pleated mechanism by which both back legs and the frame could be extended. The playing surface often had dished recesses to hold candlesticks, counters, and coins.

The growing interest in neoclassicism resulted in the popular rectangular shape being superseded by tables with D-shaped tops, often with crossbanding or marquetry decoration. Some Regency tables were fitted with a well for backgammon, above which was a reversible sliding top with a leather panel on one side and an inlaid checkerboard on the other. In the 19th century, card tables

GEORGE III HARLEQUIN MAHOGANY GAME TABLE

Twin flap tops, with rosewood and satinwood crossbanding and inlay of ebonized lines. Some versions of this table, illustrated in Sheraton's Drawing Book of 1794, have drop-flaps; they are known as harlequin Pembroke tables.

Ivory counters for backgammon, chess pieces, and dice could be stored inside the table.

Leather-lined castors facilitate the movement of these heavy tables.

Removable backgammon section. Some harlequin table were designed as dressing tab and have a specially designe interior in this section.

The superstructure of pigeonholes and drawers, also known as a "harlequin" o "till," rises by means of a series of spring and weights. The idea for mechanical tables of this type was conceived in France. It is more satisfying to find a table with its original mechanisms, but such tables must "work," so repair and replacement are often inevitable.

had a swivel and hinge mechanism, with the opened top supported by the table frame.

During the early 19th century, many card tables had a central column support, but by mid-century this had evolved into an ornamental pillar support which "sat" on a central platform or stretcher.

GEORGE I MAHOGANY TRIPLE-FLAP CARD TABLE
This table, which can serve as a game, card, or tea table, dates from the 1720s and has a fifth leg which swings out to support the opened flaps. The second flap is baize-lined for card playing while the third, seen here, is inlaid as a backgammon board and a chessboard. There is a well below for storing cards and chess pieces.

Central removable slide with a chessboard inlaid on one side; the other could be used for writing. The till could be raised when this flap was pulled forward, thereby forming a writing table.

The rectangular legs are slightly sturdier than those usually found on tables of this date. They need to be stronger than normal to carry the weight of the fixtures and mechanisms.

GEORGE II MAHOGANY CARD TABLE
Candlesticks were usually placed on the four dished square corners – sometimes called turrets – of game tables to provide illumination, while counters or money were placed in the wells. Velvet and needlework were used to line the playing surface before baize became more usual in the early 18th century. Both fabrics and baize wear, so replacement is common and does not significantly affect the value of a piece. This table may have been made in Ireland.

GEORGE III SATINWOOD CARD TABLE
Such tables were normally made in pairs and designed to stand against the wall when not in use. One of the pair had a polished top when open and could be used as a tea table; the other was baize-lined for playing cards.

TEA TABLES AND STANDS

Although tea had been a popular society drink in Britain since the late 17th century, it was not until the reign of George II that receiving friends at home to drink tea became fashionable. Tea tables with fold-over tops, similar to card tables, proliferated in the 18th and 19th centuries, as did a whole range of small tables, many of which could be stored below the tea table; larger tables with tilt tops stood at the side of the room when they were not in use.

The types of these small tables most familiar today evolved in the second quarter of the 18th century and developed from the candlestands of the 17th century; like them, they stood on tripod legs. These little tables all played a part in the tea ritual: some were used as stands for cups or glasses, others as stands on which a silver kettle and its burner could be placed. Table tops were either recessed with a raised edge or plain with a rounded edge. Most carved decoration on these tables is found on the column and legs. This is particularly true of those with plainer tops which would have been covered with a cloth when the table was in use.

A dumbwaiter is a tiered version of the tripod table, with three graduated circular trays supported by a central column. Dumbwaiters have been used since the 1720s to hold food, wines, and china for guests to help themselves when parties continued after the servants had been dismissed. Circular dumbwaiters remained popular into the 19th century, when square and rectangular versions were also made.

Many of the objects placed on dumbwaiters were heavy so it is not unusual to find splits in the wood of circular trays supported only by the central column. They should not be found on the more collectable drop-flap examples which have struts to support the open leaves.

GEORGE II MAHOGANY SUPPER TABLE

The top of this table is recessed and carved from one piece of wood. Tables such as this with eight or more carved circular recesses in which to place dishes or plates are known as supper tables after a Chippendale design.

Some supper tables have a carved scalloped edge that resembles the edge of a pie and are known as piecrust tables. Reproductions have veneered tops and the – often piecrust – rims are applied. While most tables have a circular top, examples with rectangular or square tops were also made.

Carving is common on the knees of these tables; the less usual brass inlay suggests that the table may be by John Channon, who used this technique.

The turned baluster is a common feature, as are the scrolled legs.

Pad feet, as here, as well as ball and claw and hoof feet, were all used in the 18th century. Some tables have carved legs in the form of a man's breeches, garters, and shoes; they are known as "Manx" tables after the emblem of the Isle of Man.

Feet on these tables are vulnerable – check the wood and carving to make sure restorations are sympathetic.

Engraved armorial cartouche in the center of the carved top. Some plain 18th-century tables were adapted into supper tables – the carving on "adaptations" will be less crisp than on a period table and incised, rather than standing above the surface.

Carved recess to hold one place setting.

GEORGE III KINGWOOD URN TABLE

This little table on which a silver tea urn would have stood is similar to the *tables à café* made by such French *ébénistes* as BVRB. A little drawer is fitted on this example, but some urn tables have a pull-out slide on which a tea bowl or cup could be placed.

GEORGE III TRIPOD TABLE

The spirally turned baluster stem and gadrooned knop are typical of the George III era; by the Regency period, variations were being made to this design. Here the molded circular top with its brass-inlaid spindle gallery is supported by three downswept cabriole legs joined by a shaped undertier.

This table has a tilt top which rises vertically so that the table can be stored in the corner of a room. Some table tops can also be rotated.

GEORGE III FRUITWOOD DUMBWAITER

This three-tier dumbwaiter has an urn-shaped support and cabriole legs with brass castors. Dumbwaiters sometimes lose their top tiers, with the result that the remaining one- or two-tiered table is converted into a tripod table. In-filling after the removal of the central column should be obvious on such tables. The height may also be wrong; most period tables are 27–31 inches (69–79 cm) high – treat one smaller than 24 inches (61 cm) with suspicion.

TORCHÈRES AND GUERIDONS

Candlestands were known in England and North America as torchères and in France by the wider term gueridon, which embraces any small occasional table on which candles could be stood. They evolved from the metal standards which held torches or candles and were used as lights in the Middle Ages, and the earliest English examples date from the second half of the 17th century. By the late 1600s, a pair of candlestands often formed part of a set of furniture which also included a wall mirror and side table.

Torchères and gueridons, which vary in height from the small wooden tripod-table type at about 30 inches (76 cm) to more than 50 inches (127 cm), remained popular throughout the 18th century in England and America, with their designs following the fashion of the day. By the latter part of the century, the basic shape had changed from the early columnar design to the neoclassically inspired tripod form.

A particularly popular Italian type of torchère was the blackamoor, of which many 18th- and 19th-century examples exist. These turbanned figures, holding a tray on which to stand the light, are still being made in the traditional manner today.

PAIR OF GEORGE III GILTWOOD TRIPOD TORCHÈRES

Pierced carving from the 18th century always tapers inward underneath to emphasize the illusion of lightness. The edges of period carving show signs of patination where dirt and wax has built up.

Head of Apollo, the sun god and leader of the Muses, held to be responsible for artistic inspiration.

Carved figure of a putto holding laurel branches.

Carved heads of nymphs, draped in fabric pinned at the shoulders by rosettes.

Triangular marble plinth tops were skillfully incorporated later, no doubt to add extra height. Alterations of this type to important or unusual pieces such as this do not detract from their value.

Draped urn in the center the pedestal.

Flower head carvings adorn the angles of the plinth.

The fluted guilloche plinth edges are derived from an illustration of a Greek temple in Antiquities of Athens, published in 1762.

The original gilding was burnished and applied by the water-gilding method, in which the gold leaf is put onto the surface with water. This is the only way that a burnished and flat finish can be achieved. Water gilding is less durable than oil gilding, which means that these torchères have been regilded at some stage of their history.

Sways of flower heads link the three sections of the support.

The three feathered plumes on the legs represent the insignia of the Prince of Wales. These torchères were part of a set of four supplied for the prince's use at the Queen's House (now Buckingham Palace) in late 1781. The original bill survives.

The backs of the legs are lined with metal "to keep the whole from trembling." These torchères would have been used to hold candelabra or vases of flowers and so needed to stand firm.

Satyr's *oof feet.*

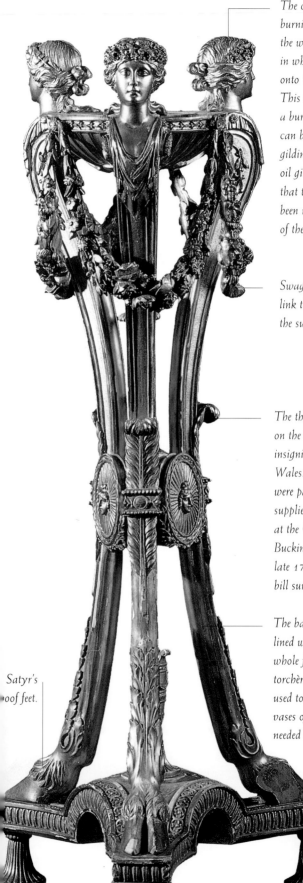

Reeded and banded feet.

PATINATED BRONZE GUERIDON
Most probably made in a Naples foundry in the second half of the 19th century, this table in the "antique" style is one of a pair of copies of braziers discovered at Pompeii and Herculaneum and exhibited at the Royal Museum in Naples. It has a circular top, paneled frieze, and slightly splayed paw feet. The tripods feature in a catalog issued by the Chiurazzi foundry in 1900.

LOUIS XV TULIPWOOD, KINGWOOD, AND MARQUETRY GUERIDON
Although still an elegant table, this gueridon has been altered since it was first made – the leather spines, which are also found on 18th-century tambour fronts, are later additions, since the books have English titles. The interior has been changed by removing the original drawer, and the ormolu mounts are also of a later date. It bears the stamp G. PÉRIDIEZ, indicating that it is the work of Gérad Péridiez, who was active in the 1760s.

GEORGE III ORMOLU-MOUNTED PAINTED LAMP TABLE
The canted top of this painted table is inset with a Bartolozzi print in the style of a painting of bathing putti by G.B. Cipriani. Florentine-born Cipriani went to England in 1755 and was one of the first exponents of neoclassicism there. The table stands on ring-turned tapering legs joined by arched X-stretchers. There was originally an apron beneath the frieze.

OCCASIONAL TABLES

As smaller rooms became increasingly common in the 18th century, so demand grew for tables that did not fit the late 17th-century models of side or center tables. Hence the occasional table, a small table designed for general use and to serve a variety of functions.

French *ébénistes* supplied a variety of small tables (known as *tables ambulantes*) for every conceivable purpose, often combining more than one use. Their decoration was almost as varied, with porcelain, ormolu, marquetry, gilding, and carving all used to great effect. Popular designs have been copied ever since. Among the various forms of English occasional tables is the china table, also known as a tea or silver table. Usually rectangular in shape, such tables have a pierced fretwork gallery to prevent objects from being knocked off accidentally.

Marble became a particularly popular material for table tops in the 19th century. Visitors to Italy on the Grand Tour were impressed by table tops which were inlaid with various specimens of marble, precious stones, and even micromosaics and pietra dura. Such tops were often mounted on bases when the travelers returned home. Specimen tables with tops containing native hard stones also exist.

SET OF QUARTETTO TABLES BY GEORGE OAKLEY

Many quartetto tables – sets of four – as here, rely on the graining of the woods used, usually mahogany, for decorative effect; later examples have painted decoration, often neoclassical in inspiration. Papier-mâché examples were also made in the 19th century.

Star motif brass inlay. During the Regency period, brass inlay became a fashionable decoration in furniture design and was particularly popular with dark woods. Here it is used with calamander and ebony.

Concave stretchers and downswept tapering feet fit together perfectly.

Singles or pairs of these tables are quite often found, but it is obvious from their proportions and the way that they do not fit snugly that they were once part of a bigger set.

Knowledge of a piece of furniture's history is always a bonus and can enhance its value. These tables were supplied to a Cambridgeshire family in 1810 and remained its property through successive generations, until they were sold in the early 1990s.

RUSSIAN OCCASIONAL TABLE
The top of this ormolu-mounted amaranth and kingwood marquetry table, which dates from the late 18th century, is inlaid with a neoclassical urn. And there are stylistically similar decorative devices on the ormolu band above the molded frieze. The square tapering legs end in brass castors – a useful feature on a table designed to be moved around a room and used for a variety of purposes.

A similar table, made in St. Petersburg, and with an established provenance, has a *verre églomisé* top.

Corners are particularly vulnerable on such delicate tables, but sympathetic restoration or replacement of veneer does not detract from the value of such a set.

PORTUGUESE SIDE TABLE
Panels from a 16th-century Goanese cabinet have been incorporated into the top of this table. Such additions, which are not confined to tables, are obvious from the style of both addition and piece of furniture, and can enhance a piece's curiosity value. Turned legs, here bobbin-turned, united by shaped X-stretchers, are typical features of many side and center tables made in Europe in the late 17th century.

Period sets always have good proportions; later copies are rather "spindly" by comparison. Also sometimes made in sets of three (trio tables) or five (quintetto tables), they are the forerunners of the modern nest tables.

GILTWOOD CENTER TABLE
This northern Italian table – it may have originated from the region around Venice – was made in the 19th century. However, its black- and pink-veined marble top, the giltwood base in the form of a tree trunk with disporting putti and birds, and the naturalistic base carved with rocks and foliage make it a good example of a type of occasional table that has been made from the late 17th century onward. It is a style still commonly reproduced today.

FIELDED PANEL
A flat panel with beveled edges
that fits into grooves in the
framing rail without glue, to allow
the wood to swell or shrink.

HINGED TOP
Early chests had a top or
lid that could be opened
to reach the articles
stored inside.

PAINTING
Decoration worked with paint on
a piece of furniture; used on both
provincial and more upmarket
pieces (see pp. 142–45).

BLIND DOOR
A door made completely of
wood so that the contents of
the piece of furniture are not
visible when it is shut.
Glazed doors, by contrast,
do allow the interior and
contents to be viewed when
the doors are shut.

STILE
Vertical member of a
framework placed at the end
or corner of a piece of
paneled furniture.

ROCOCO HANDLE
The rococo style was
characterized by gentle
curves and often
asymmetrical motifs.

BANDING
A strip of wood
inlaid into another
of contrasting color
or grain direction,
used as decoration.

LOCK
Most 18th-century
chests of drawers were
fitted with locks.

DUSTBOARD
The thin piece of
wood separating the
drawers in a chest,
intended to prevent
contents from catching
on the drawer above,
and for security and
dust prevention.

ORMOLU SABOT
Sabots (meaning
hooves) were used on
the feet of some case
furniture to protect the
veneers on the leg.

ESCUTCHEON
The shaped plate
around a keyhole,
which helps protect
the wood from being
damaged by the key.

MOUNT
A decorative device,
often of ormolu,
added to a piece of
furniture.

CHESTS & CHESTS OF DRAWERS

Practical and decorative, chests vary in style from the simple bow-fronted chest of drawers which graced most 19th-century homes to the elaborate ormolu-mounted lacquer commode made by Martin Carlin for Louis XVI's aunts. Both served a purpose: the former as a functional piece of storage furniture, the latter as a symbol of its owners' rank and an indicator of their taste.

Chests vary enormously in shape and size from the small, low coffer to the large tallboy or chest-on-chest.

Those made by leading cabinetmakers might be decorated with matched veneers, marquetry, parquetry, or painted finishes. Chests have always been popular, and many period examples of all types survive and continue to give pleasure today. This enduring popularity has also meant that early designs have often been copied, with many copies now antiques in their own right. A number are still reproduced, but today's smaller homes usually mean that modern copies are smaller than the originals they emulate.

PEDIMENT
Surmounts the cornice in cabinet furniture. Popular forms are the swan neck and broken arch.

CARVING
A design or figure worked into wood, either at the time of making, or applied later.

DRAWER
Until the mid-18th century, the grain of wood used on drawer bottoms ran from front to back; on later drawers it runs from side to side.

MOLDING
A shaped decorative piece of wood applied to furniture, sometimes used to hide a joint.

OGEE BRACKET FOOT
Double curved shape, convex at the top, and concave at the bottom, sometimes found on the feet of case furniture. See pp. 108–9.

DROP
A carved ornament.

OTHER USEFUL TERMS

CASE FURNITURE A piece of furniture designed to contain something, for example, a chest of drawers, bureau, or bureau bookcase.

COCKBEADING A thin molding applied to the edge of a drawer to prevent damage to the veneer when the drawer is opened and shut.

FINIAL A decorative ornament, projecting upward, found on the top of tall case furniture.

MIDMOLDING The molding between the top and bottom sections of a chest-on-chest.

PILASTER Partial column on the face of a piece of furniture, often rectangular in section.

PLINTH A solid base section used instead of legs on cabinet furniture.

RUNNER The rectangular piece of wood attached to a carcass along which a corresponding groove in the side of a drawer slides; in the 18th century, the sides of a drawer projected below its base and acted as runners.

VENEER A thin sheet of wood applied over a carcass for decorative effect.

DESIGN DETAILS

There are several elements that may help in looking at and dating chests and chests of drawers. Most made since the late 17th century are of case construction in which sides, back, and drawers are all fitted in a basic frame. This carcass may have been veneered: hand-cut veneers are usually at least ⅛ inch (3 mm) thick; machine-cut ones are much thinner. An examination of a drawer's dovetails will reveal whether they have been cut by hand or machine.

The wood used for drawer linings, the way the grain runs, and how the drawers fit together and fit into the carcass also help to establish age, as do overall shape and the style of feet used. Handles are not always reliable indicators as they are often replaced, but it is useful to know the correct style for a certain date. Finally, decorative details can also be helpful.

Feet and castors

Bun foot
1680–1710

Ball foot
1690–1730

Bracket foot
1720–80

Bracket foot
1720–80

Ogee foot
1740–75

Newport ball and claw
1750–80

Splay foot
1780–1810

Turned
foot 1850

Turned foot
1870

Brass with
leather disks
1740–50

Square
1760–75

Box or
bullnose
1780

Square box
1780

Tapered
socket
1780–1800

Lion's paw
1780–1830

Regency
foliate box
1800–1830

Handles

Early drop
17th century

Simple loop
17th century

Split tail
1690–1710

Queen Anne drop
1700–1720

Swan neck with pierced
backplate
1740–60

Swan neck with pierced
backplate
1740–60

Chinese Chippendale
1750–1780

Swan neck
1770–80

Oval with swag motif
1780–1800

Squared
1780–1800

Round handle with
floral backplate
1790–1830

Regency lion
1820–1830

Porcelain
1840–60

Wood with decorative
inset
1840–60

Locks and keyholes

Bramah lock,
patented in 1784.

The simplest escutcheons are
linings to the keyhole, usually
made of brass.

Rounded
escutcheon
1850s

English
escutcheon
1870

Drawer fronts may have filled-in holes inside
where the drawer has been reduced in width,
or where handles have been changed.

Construction

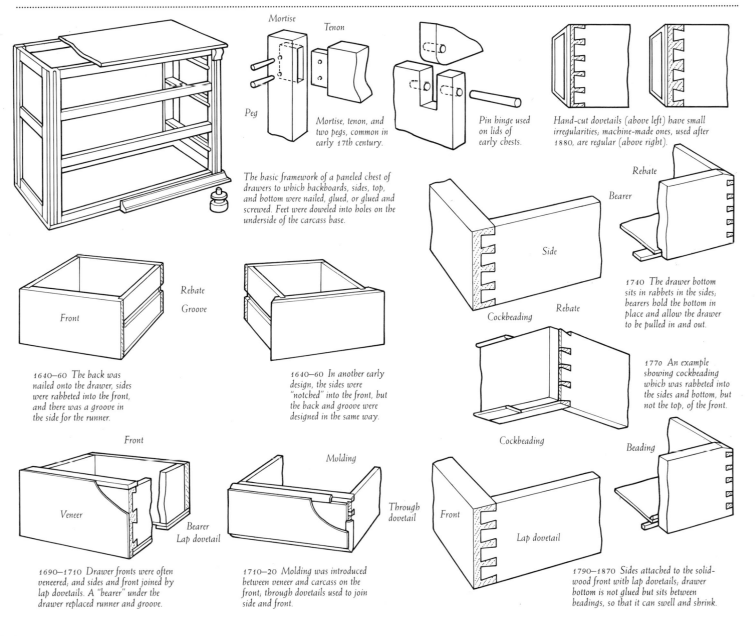

Mortise

Tenon

Peg

Mortise, tenon, and two pegs, common in early 17th century.

Pin hinge used on lids of early chests.

Hand-cut dovetails (above left) have small irregularities; machine-made ones, used after 1880, are regular (above right).

The basic framework of a paneled chest of drawers to which backboards, sides, top, and bottom were nailed, glued, or glued and screwed. Feet were doweled into holes on the underside of the carcass base.

Rebate

Bearer

Side

Cockbeading

Rebate

1740 The drawer bottom sits in rabbets in the sides; bearers hold the bottom in place and allow the drawer to be pulled in and out.

Rebate

Front

Groove

1640–60 The back was nailed onto the drawer, sides were rabbeted into the front, and there was a groove in the side for the runner.

1640–60 In another early design, the sides were "notched" into the front, but the back and groove were designed in the same way.

1770 An example showing cockbeading which was rabbeted into the sides and bottom, but not the top, of the front.

Front

Veneer

Bearer
Lap dovetail

1690–1710 Drawer fronts were often veneered; and sides and front joined by lap dovetails. A "bearer" under the drawer replaced runner and groove.

Molding

Through dovetail

1710–20 Molding was introduced between veneer and carcass on the front; through dovetails used to join side and front.

Cockbeading

Front

Lap dovetail

Beading

1790–1870 Sides attached to the solid-wood front with lap dovetails; drawer bottom is not glued but sits between beadings, so that it can swell and shrink.

Chest shapes

Bombé, 1750.
The term means "with a bulging, rounded lower front."

Serpentine, 1750.
The term means "with a double-curved outline."

Bow front
1780–1800.

COFFERS AND CHESTS

The earliest known piece of furniture – with ancient Egyptian examples still in existence – is the rectangular top-opening coffer, or chest. The earliest European coffers were hollowed out from tree trunks, and it was not until the 13th century that they were made from planks nailed together, and in some cases banded with iron for additional strength. During the 15th century, European makers developed new construction techniques, and chests were made of paneled or jointed construction using mortise and tenon joints. On such chests, which were made without glue, expect some movement of the panels. Coffers were almost always intended to be portable and were used for the storage of valuable items in addition to clothing; those used as strongboxes are often fitted with very elaborate locks.

Coffers have a major drawback, however: it is difficult to reach things stored at the bottom. To help overcome this, some 17th-century chests were made with one or two drawers in their base. Since they combine elements of both the coffer and the chest of drawers, they are generically known as mule chests. Coffers continued to be made for a long time after chests of drawers became popular, especially in rural areas.

16TH-CENTURY FRENCH WALNUT CASSONE

The cassone shape originated in Renaissance Italy – the design is based on the sarcophagi of ancient Rome. Cassoni were often made as marriage chests and were highly decorated with either painted scenes or inlay. They were also reproduced in the 19th century.

The hinged rectangular top of a coffer could be used either as a seat or as a table top. Expect the interior wood to have a dry appearance.

Carvings of mythological scenes, herms (representations of the head of Hermes, messenger of the gods), and swagged drapery – all Renaissance features that were adopted from Italy by French craftsmen in the 16th century – decorate the twin front panels.

Both apron and feet, although stylistically correct, are later additions. Coffers underwent a period of renewed popularity in Victorian times, with additional motifs carved or added to an existing coffer; new coffers were also made up from old pieces of wood.

OAK COFFER

Dating in part from the 15th and 16th centuries, this coffer has a front panel carved with typical Gothic tracery and quatrefoils. Feet on coffers of this form are a continuous part of the stiles, so replacements are obvious. Original feet will be worn down.

Carving on Victorian reproductions has none of the restraint of period carving; original carving also stands away from the surface. Later additions are often incised.

Gadrooning, reeding, or fluting, either molded or carved, decorates the top edge.

Carrying handles were added to the sides of most types of coffers to make them easy to transport.

VENETIAN CEDARWOOD COFFER

Dating from the first half of the 17th century, by which time coffers often had one single large front panel, this coffer has an incised and inlaid design, although they were often still carved. The bracket feet are later in date; this is not uncommon and, as long as they look "right," has little significance.

GERMAN WALNUT COFFER

Coffers were still made after the chest of drawers had evolved. They were used to store linens and clothes, including those which formed part of a bride's dowry, hence the name dower chest. This trunk-shaped example dates from the early 18th century.

CHESTS OF DRAWERS

Among the most practical pieces of furniture, chests of drawers were once so popular that there was normally at least one in every room – which is why antique examples are still plentiful today.

The basic chest of drawers shape had evolved in England by about 1650. Such chests were of frame and panel construction, but European craftsmen, who followed Charles II to England after the Restoration in 1660, introduced a new method that gradually replaced this traditional way of working. This was case construction, in which the carcass of a piece of furniture was dovetailed together from a "cheap" wood such as pine or oak, and then veneered with a better-quality wood such as walnut.

Many chests made during this period were decorated with parquetry and marquetry. By the time of Queen Anne, however, more importance was placed on matching the wood's figuring in the walnut veneers – both along individual drawer fronts and between the fronts on a chest – for decorative effect.

In the 18th century, French styles and forms influenced much European furniture design, but rectangular chests of drawers remained popular in England until mid-century, when the French-inspired serpentine shape found favor there and elsewhere. By the 1770s, bow-fronted chests were being made, and like rectangular shapes, they remained popular into the next century. In the 19th century, pine was commonly used for chests made for the poorer classes while those made for richer buyers were of mahogany.

CHIPPENDALE CARVED MAHOGANY CHEST OF DRAWERS

The drawers are graduated. By the late 17th century, runners were attached to the sides of a chest and corresponding grooves, or rabbets, in the drawer sides (running front to back) made drawers easier to slide in and out. After 1710, a different type became the norm. The sides and front of the drawer extended below its base, with the sides acting as runners.

A sliding shelf between the chest top and first drawer features on many English chests. Called a brushing slide, it could be pulled out and have clothes laid on it for brushing.

The blockfront construction of this chest, made in Massachusetts between 1760 and 1780, is also found in European furniture.

The carved scallop-shell motif on the block front is a typically American feature.

The handles are probably original. On many chests, of whatever period, the handles have been changed by later generations to make the chest seem more up-to-date in style; more recently, the reverse has happened. Such changes are apparent on the inside – there will be filled-in holes.

QUEEN ANNE WALNUT BACHELOR'S CHEST
Early 18th-century chests of drawers, bachelor's chests are shallow and have a hinged top that folds forward to form a table surface. When opened, the top is supported by lopers that slide out, as on a desk – these are visible in the top corners of the front of the chest. Because of their small size – this chest is only 35 inches (89 cm) high – such chests are popular and much copied. Many larger period chests have been reduced in size.

A molded edge is common on the carved top.

Dustboards are usual between the drawers. They remained popular until the 20th century when side runners again came into vogue, this time often without boards between the drawers.

KINGWOOD AND TULIPWOOD SEMAINIER
As the name suggests, a semainier – an 18th-century French chest of drawers – has up to seven drawers, supposedly one for each day of the week. This one is stamped with the name CHEVALLIER. The early 19th-century English Wellington chests are similar, but were used to house collector's items such as coins and medals. Wellington chests have a hinged right-hand column that must be unlocked and opened before the drawers can be pulled out.

MILITARY CHEST
Often made of mahogany or teak, military chests usually have brass-bound corners and recessed handles. This example has a central secrétaire drawer at the top and is in two sections for ease of carrying. The style, which is still reproduced, found favor in the Regency and early Victorian periods, and many chests were made for household – rather than military – use.

The bracket feet are original and of ogee shape (a double curve, convex at the top and concave at the bottom).

COMMODES

Richly decorated chests of drawers made to stand in a salon or drawing room, commodes evolved in early 18th-century France and soon spread from France to the rest of Europe. In all countries, great attention was paid to the making of these prestigious pieces of furniture, often in the latest style, as they were regarded as status symbols. Commodes have either drawers or doors which open to reveal drawers or shelves. Their decoration is varied, with parquetry, marquetry, painting, porcelain or *pietra dura* panels, boullework, and gilt-metal mounts among the many devices and materials used.

In England, although known as "French commodes," they were usually made with a wooden top, rather than the marble top preferred by the French. English commodes first appeared in the 1740s and early examples were often bombé or serpentine in outline, but later in the century many had bow fronts and by the time of the Regency they were more often rectangular.

Commodes continued to be popular throughout the 19th century in many European countries. Pastiches of earlier shapes and decorations proliferated, but exact copies – perhaps varying in only decorative detail – of important 18th-century pieces were also common.

Beneath the marble top of many commodes the maker's mark may be found. After 1741 Parisian ébénistes were required to put their stamp on the furniture they made, which was also marked by their guild "JME" (Juré des Menuisiers et Ebénistes) to show that it had approved the work. Stylistically, this commode resembles the work of Levasseur jeune, although the true maker is unknown.

SÈVRES-INLAID COMMODE

The plaques are of 18th-century Sèvres porcelain (c.1765), reused from an earlier piece. The practice of using porcelain plaques to decorate furniture originated in the 18th century; and some ébénistes such as BVRB, RVLC, and Martin Carlin specialized in producing furniture with this type of decoration. Much 19th-century furniture has plaques in the Sèvres style as decoration.

Breakfront centered by ormolu drop.

Tapering leg inlaid with bellflowers.

Foliate plaques decorate the corners.

Side inlaid with trellis and rosette design in shaded woods.

Original top of Carrara marble. Replacements are common, either because of accidental damage or because the commode was moved to another room and the top changed to match the marble of the fireplace. Such changes could have happened in the 18th century or later, but are less common on later pieces.

GEORGE III MARQUETRY AND CROSSBANDED COMMODE
The serpentine shape of this commode owes much to French designs, while the amaranth, kingwood, and satinwood marquetry reflects rococo influences in the flowers on the inside of the door. The classical urns, part of the design on the door fronts, show the trend toward the neoclassical style.

Attractive ormolu mounts. The word ormolu derives from the French for ground gold and refers to mounts of bronze, brass, or other metals which have been gilded. The term gilt bronze is used for 18th-century mounts gilded by the mercury process, which was made illegal in the mid-19th century because of the noxious fumes involved.

COMMODE EN TOMBEAU
A 19th-century copy of the renowned pair of commodes made for Louis XIV by A.-C. Boulle in 1709, this is one of the earliest designs for a type of commode. The brass-inlaid tortoiseshell is typical of Boulle's furniture, the style of which became fashionable again in the late 18th century and remained popular through the 19th century.

This rectangular breakfront form is in Louis XVI style, which became popular again during the 19th century; this commode was made about 1840.

ITALIAN WALNUT COMMODE
The bombé shape of this piece was popular throughout Europe in the mid-18th century. The asymmetrical rococo shape of the handles and escutcheons of the drawers is typical. The cabriole legs are later replacements, but the originals would have been of a similar style.

CHESTS-ON-CHESTS AND PRESSES

A European invention that found its way to England after the Restoration, a chest-on-stand is literally a chestlike superstructure on a low stand, usually with baluster legs joined by wavy stretchers. The top of the chest section was not normally veneered.

By the early 18th century, chests-on-stands had been replaced by the more practical chest-on-chest, or tallboy. As with chests-on-stands, the two sections could be separated if necessary. Early tallboys were of veneered walnut or burl walnut, but by the 1740s, mahogany veneers were being used. In the early 18th century, tallboys were rectangular in shape, but later in the century they were also made with either serpentine or bow fronts. They declined in popularity early in the 19th century.

Chests-on-stands were popular in the United States from the end of the 17th until well into the 18th century. Known as "highboys," they were important items in the cabinetmaker's repertoire. Their stands resembled "lowboys," or dressing tables, and lowboys were sometimes made to match highboys.

Linen or clothes presses, which became increasingly popular from the mid-18th century onward, have a tall cabinet with two doors enclosing an interior fitted with sliding shelves, which sits on a chest-of-drawers base. Some early 19th century presses were made with cupboards for hanging clothes, flanking the traditionally arranged central section; these pieces were the obvious forerunners of the armoire.

CARVED MAHOGANY BLOCKFRONT CHEST-ON-CHEST

The fan carving is a typical detail found on furniture produced in Massachusetts.

Proportionately graduated drawers in both top and bottom sections are common.

The pilasters are a further indication that this is the work of a Massachusetts cabinetmaker. It was made to a Chippendale design between 1760 and 1790.

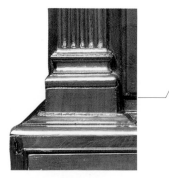

The joint between top and bottom is usually apparent, but carving should flow from one to the other. Treat interrupted lines with suspicion.

Ogee bracket feet.

Flame finial.

The bonnet-top carved pediment can be found on highboys, tallboys, and bookcases. Bonnet tops flourished in the United States, but were not popular in Britain.

Three drawers across the top of such pieces are usual.

The open spaces on each side of the center of the pediment can help identify where a piece was made. The circular shape seen here indicates that this chest-on-chest was made in New England.

The lower chest has a block front.

Handles and escutcheons are typical of American Chippendale pieces; on English examples they are less ornate.

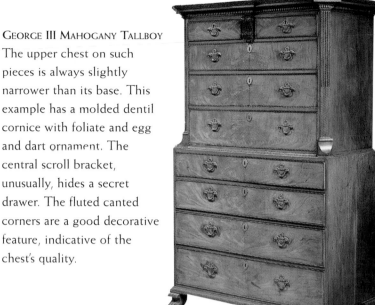

GEORGE III MAHOGANY TALLBOY
The upper chest on such pieces is always slightly narrower than its base. This example has a molded dentil cornice with foliate and egg and dart ornament. The central scroll bracket, unusually, hides a secret drawer. The fluted canted corners are a good decorative feature, indicative of the chest's quality.

WALNUT CABINET-ON-CHEST
This piece is a "marriage," more usual with chests-on-chests. Here a late 17th-century chest from a chest-on-stand has been put onto an 18th-century base to make a more useful piece of furniture. When tallboys fell from favor, they were often split into two chests of drawers. Today, two chests of drawers are more likely to be united.

GEORGE III PALISANDER SERPENTINE CLOTHES PRESS
In two separate sections and fitted with carrying handles, usual for presses of this type, this is from a Chippendale design for a "commode clothes press," first published in 1753. The interior is fitted with four trays for storing clothes and linens.

LACQUER
A black resinous substance obtained from a tree of the sumach family, *Rhus vernicifera*, used to give a hard glossy finish to wooden furniture.

HINGE
On some pieces of case furniture, hinges are elaborately shaped and decorated.

PILASTER
Partial column on the face of a piece of furniture, often rectangular in section.

INLAY
A decoration of contrasting wood, bone, shell, brass, or ivory inset into solid wood.

OTHER USEFUL TERMS

BREAKFRONT The protruding center section on a sideboard and other pieces of furniture, popular in the 18th and 19th centuries.

CELLARET See pp. 8–11 and 78–79.

KNIFEBOX See pp. 78–79.

PLINTH A solid base section used instead of legs on cabinet furniture.

SHELF A flat rectangular piece of wood on which items can be stored in a cupboard or cabinet.

BUN FOOT
Similar to the ball foot, the bun foot is slightly flattened. It was a popular design in the second half of the 17th century.

BLIND DOOR
A door made entirely of wood or other solid material so that the contents of a piece cannot be seen when the door is shut. Glazed doors, by contrast, allow a piece's interior and contents to be viewed when they are shut.

MOLDING
A shaped decorative piece of wood applied to furniture, sometimes used to hide joints.

FRIEZE DRAWER
A drawer in the frieze or framework below the top.

STAND
The sometimes highly decorated wooden frame on legs supporting a cabinet or chest.

STRETCHER
The horizontal strut connecting the legs of cabinet stands, tables, or chairs. Here it is baluster turned.

TURNED LEG
The legs of many such stands incorporate turned decoration. Here they are baluster or vase, turned.

CUPBOARDS, CABINETS, & DRESSERS

Adequate means of storage – for food, clothes, and valuables – has long been a requisite of daily life, and every household has at least one sort of cupboard, often a sideboard or hutch, sometimes a corner cupboard or display cabinet. Storage furniture has been made since medieval times. Many of the pieces intended for town dwellers were made to follow the latest fashions, but country furniture was made in traditional styles long after these had been abandoned by city cabinetmakers.

The archetypal individual pieces of storage furniture did not "happen" overnight, but evolved over a period of years and, in some cases, centuries. Sideboards, for example, developed from medieval serving tables into the basic shape that is instantly recognizable today, regardless of whether the stylistic details added by the cabinetmaker classify it as Chippendale or Victorian. In a similar manner, display or corner cupboards are descended from the small transportable cabinets used in the 16th century to hold valuable coins or papers safely. Today, such cabinets tend to hold a houschold's "best" china and glass – the basic form remains the same, but design is dictated by fashion, and function by way of life.

REGENCY LION HANDLE
[Typ]e of handle used in the early [1]9th century, in which the ring [p]ull protrudes from the mouth of a lion.

SPIRAL TURNING
Turning was used on high-quality furniture, as well as on country and provincial pieces.

BACK RAIL
A brass rail from which a curtain was hung to prevent the wall from being splashed when food was served.

APRON
The lower front edge of a piece of furniture; here it is arched.

ESCUTCHEON
The shaped plate around a keyhole, which helps protect the wood from being damaged by the key.

CORNICE
Top molding or decorative projection on tall cabinet furniture.

DRAWER
Based on the court cupboard, some early American cupboards have one long drawer; others, as here, have two. Carved decoration is common.

BALUSTER
A shaped, turned piece of wood usually used as a support.

BOTTLE DRAWER
A deep drawer in a sideboard in which bottles could be stored.

FIELDED PANEL
A flat panel with beveled edges that fits into grooves in the framing rail without glue, to allow the wood to swell or shrink.

MUNTIN
The vertical framework between panels.

DESIGN DETAILS

The term cupboards, cabinets, and dressers or hutches cover such a variety of dining room furniture that identifying the major characteristics of a particular piece can be difficult. The chart below defines the major types. It is important to remember that many such pieces, like the hutch, have fallen from favor only to be revived years later, a factor that can make dating difficult.

Pieces may also have been altered: many oriental cabinets were placed on special stands, so identifying the stylistic features of a stand can be helpful in dating the cabinet, but there is no guarantee that cabinet and stand have always belonged together.

Wine coolers and bottle stands

Knife cases

Sarcophagus-shaped
wine cooler
1830

Wine cooler, George II 1750

Bottle stand, George II
1750

Bottle stand, Irish
1760

Cellaret, South
Carolina
1795–1805

Cellaret, Boston
1805–10

English knife case
1775

English country
knife box
1790

George III knife box
1790

Styles and definitions

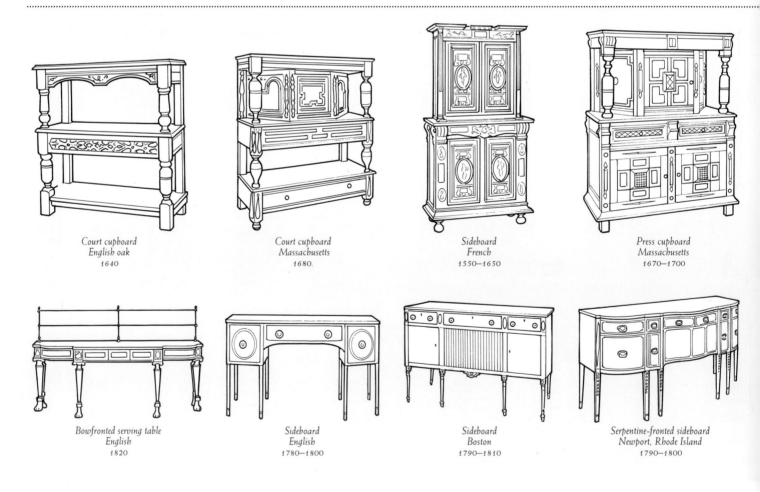

Court cupboard
English oak
1640

Court cupboard
Massachusetts
1680.

Sideboard
French
1550–1650

Press cupboard
Massachusetts
1670–1700

Bowfronted serving table
English
1820

Sideboard
English
1780–1800

Sideboard
Boston
1790–1810

Serpentine-fronted sideboard
Newport, Rhode Island
1790–1800

Stands

Finishes

English, 1670

Spanish, 1650

English, 1800–20

English, 1700

New York, 1700

American, 1700

Flemish, 1650

North German, 1720

English, 1850

Sideboard
English
1780–1800

Linen press
New York, based on English designs
1785–95

Sideboard table
English
1780

Sideboard
Philadelphia
1870

Sideboard
New York, influenced by Charles Eastlake
1875–80

Credenza
English
1860

Boulle

Marble

Gilt strapwork

Ormolu

Sèvres plaque

Ivory inlay

Pietra dura

Parcel-gilt

Lacquer

COURT CUPBOARDS

On special occasions in the Middle Ages, a family displayed its silver plate on a series of stepped platforms, but by the Elizabethan era, a piece of furniture known as a "cup board," with two or three open shelves, had evolved for such purposes. The term court cupboard used to describe these pieces today derives from the French *court* (short), since they were relatively low, usually about 4 feet (1.2 m) high. This design, often featuring bulbous column supports at the front and plainer ones at the back, remained popular in England into the 17th century and was still being made in America until about 1690.

Other cupboards found in 16th- and 17th-century households were the aumbrey, which had a closed upper cupboard section with an open shelf below, and the larger press, or parlor cupboard, which consisted of two enclosed cupboards, the upper slightly shallower than its lower counterpart. Both halves were usually fitted with doors. Although these cupboards were made in many different woods, the majority of those still in existence are of oak.

In Europe during the 16th century, similar developments were taking place, including the introduction of the buffet, made in either one or two stages (two-stage models were known as *buffets à deux corps*, that is, with two bodies) and often richly decorated. It was a form that remained popular well into the 19th century.

GRENOBLE WALNUT BUFFET OR ARMOIRE

The top door panel is mid-16th century and is carved with a depiction of the destruction of Sodom and Gomorrah.

The panels with gilt arabesque designs are of slate and make a good contrast with the richness of the carved walnut.

In shape, form, and style, this piece is 16th century, but it was assembled in the 19th century using earlier elements. In the 19th and early 20th centuries, many of these types of cabinets were reproduced, made up from old fragments, or "improved" through the addition of carving.

Carving of biblical scenes adorns the lower panels.

The turned bun feet are in keeping with the overall style — round bun feet are also found. The back feet on buffets are usually different from those at the front.

Molded cornices are a common feature of the tops of tall pieces of furniture; here the cornice is of breakfront form.

LATE ELIZABETHAN OAK FOOD CUPBOARD

This cupboard is similar in shape to the open-shelved court cupboard, although these were more elaborately decorated as they were more prestigious items. The fluted baluster legs are an attractive feature. Many food cupboards have pierced panels for ventilation. In the 19th century, early pieces were copied, made up, or "improved."

Paneled outer border carved with figures symbolizing Prudence, Charity, Love, and Temptation. Such figures are typical of the mannerist style that emerged from Renaissance Italy and found favor in 16th-century France.

ENGLISH RENAISSANCE OAK CUPBOARD

Dating from the early 16th century, this cupboard was probably used to store linens and hangings. The carved heads on the doors are examples of romayne work, a decorative feature widely used on 16th-century furniture and paneling. Copied from Italian Renaissance designs, romayne work is a medallioned head in profile within a roundel. Other carved motifs here include scrolling foliage and linenfolds.

Frieze drawers with molded seraphim handles.

The molded spreading plinth is a typical feature; expect corners to show signs of wear.

SOUTH GERMAN BUFFET

This mid-18th century ebonized walnut buffet is large – it is 7 feet (2.1 m) wide and has elaborate marquetry decoration featuring a variety of figures and hunting, village, and courtly scenes. In addition to the visible drawers, there are others concealed by the cupboard doors. The back is arched and paneled.

LOW DRESSERS AND BUFFETS

In the Middle Ages, side tables were used for preparing or "dressing" food, hence the evolution of the dresser. In the 17th century, dressers were fitted with a frieze of drawers below the board, and by the early 18th century, a shelved superstructure was a feature, sometimes with backboards, and usually with a shaped cornice frieze to match the apron below the drawers. Dressers, or hutches, are, however, essentially rural pieces; wealthier homes might have one in the kitchen, but the dining room was more usually furnished with side or serving tables.

Robert Adam was probably the first designer to feature pedestals in the dining room. Standing on each side of a serving table, they could be used to store bottles or plates; the decorated urns on top contained hot or iced water, while a matching wine cooler stood beneath the table.

This arrangement of several separate items was not viable in smaller houses, and by the 1770s, the pedestals were being incorporated into the serving table to form a single piece of furniture, the forerunner of the modern sideboard. Early sideboards usually stand on six legs and have a drawer or cupboard at each end with a central drawer to hold flatware. Although there was space to stand a wine cooler beneath the

FEDERAL MAHOGANY SIDEBOARD

Sideboards vary in shape; this one is bow fronted, but serpentine and straight-fronted examples also exist. Copies of 18th-century sideboards abound, but should be easy to spot from the method of construction.

There are three drawers on the left-hand side. Very large 18th-century sideboards have sometimes been reduced in depth. Check that the runners stop short of the backboard and that all dovetails are the same.

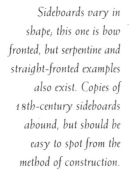

The square tapering legs end in spade feet. The turned legs of later sideboards are sometimes replaced with tapering legs to make them appear older and more valuable.

The backboard of a copy will probably be of mahogany rather than pine.

The right-hand door bears the label of the New York maker Thomas Burling.

A recessed cupboard was a popular feature in late 18th-century New England and is also found on some English sideboards, although open kneeholes and solid backboards are more common in Britain.

The central drawer has cockbeading around its edge. Cockbeading is a molding found around the edges of drawers to protect the veneer from damage. Some sideboards have crossbanding or stringing instead of cockbeading.

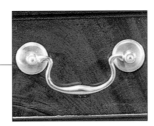

central section, one of the end drawers was often lead-lined for this purpose.

Some sideboards made in the 1790s and during the Regency period were fitted with a brass back rail from which a curtain could be hung to protect the wall from splashes when meals were being served. By the 19th century, a demand for more storage space meant that some sideboards were made with pedestal-shaped end cupboards.

Handles may be original; these are the correct style.

The right-hand side, despite its appearance, has one drawer at the top and a deep drawer for bottles below.

Applied moldings and brass handles give the impression that the right-hand side has the same number of drawers as the left.

Inlay on the legs and stiles of Federal sideboards is not uncommon; English examples may have had inlay added later to "improve" the overall appearance of the sideboard.

REGENCY EGYPTIAN-STYLE MAHOGANY PEDESTAL SIDEBOARD
The pedestal-shaped cupboards at each end are topped by knifeboxes. The left-hand pedestal is fitted with a deep drawer, while that on the right is a cupboard containing three bottle recesses. Originally this sideboard would also have had a gallery.

GEORGE III EXTENDING SERVING TABLE
Made of mahogany, this table is 6 feet (1.8 m) long when closed and 9 feet (2.7 m) long when opened. It has a rectangular breakfront top, and its central frieze is carved with a floral and ribbon swag with a rosette at the center, although the extending side friezes are plain. Classical-style urns top the square tapering legs.

GEORGE III OAK SHROPSHIRE DRESSER
There are many regional variations in dressers (hutches). This design has a frieze of three drawers below the molded top; an arcaded gallery supported by columns; and a bottom board or shelf, known as a potboard, for storing large items. This hutch originally had a superstructure.

SIDEBOARDS AND SIDE CABINETS

Pedestal-style sideboards remained popular after the Regency, but the low backboard which had become a feature toward the end of the period became higher in the Victorian era, and increasingly more decorative, with carved or painted panels or mirrors featuring in the design. Nor was the space beneath the central drawer, between the pedestals, sacrosanct: this was soon enclosed to give additional cupboard space.

As with most pieces of furniture in the Victorian age, sideboards were made in a variety of styles, both mainstream and "reformed." Arts and Crafts movement craftsmen made sideboards and hutches that influenced designers in many European countries, including Austria. In the late 19th century and the early 20th, there was a revival of interest in Georgian styles, particularly those of Chippendale and

Sheraton, which lasted until shortly before World War II.

Some side cabinets are known by the name credenza (Italian for sideboard). This is something of a misnomer since many credenzas – fitted with glazed doors so that porcelain and ornaments could be displayed – were intended for the parlor rather than the dining room. But credenzas with blind doors were used in the dining room.

LATE VICTORIAN SATINWOOD AND MARQUETRY SIDE CABINET

Bow-fronted frieze inlaid with scrolling foliage.

The locks on the doors and each set of drawers are stamped EL'S-EY GT. PORTLAND ST. LONDON. Most 18th- and 19th-century chests were fitted with locks, perhaps the best known of which are of the Bramah type, a design patented in 1784.

The tapering toupie feet are turned.

One door is stamped EDWARDS & ROBERTS, a London firm specializing in Chippendale and Sheraton revival furniture.

Marquetry decoration in the scrolling foliage on the front and on the top is more elaborate than on most period sideboards.

The painted panels on the bow-fronted doors depict Watteauesque scenes of lovers, a subject that is a typical decorative feature found on painted furniture made in the 19th century and later.

The top incorporates a fan medallion and husk and scroll inlay. Many 18th-century pieces were "improved" at this time by the addition of inlaid and painted decoration. These later alterations are usually obvious from the styling and workmanship.

LATE REGENCY MAHOGANY PEDESTAL SIDEBOARD

One of a pair, this sideboard made in about 1825 clearly shows how the pedestal style was becoming heavier in appearance. There is bronze decoration of vine leaves and clusters on the back rail, and the flattened-column pedestals end in paw feet; the frieze and capitals are decorated with gadrooning. One of the sideboards is fitted with a bottle cupboard.

Five graduated drawers flank each side of the central cupboard.

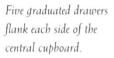

Pilasters are decorated with bell husks and have carved capitals.

PARQUETRY, WALNUT, AND OAK BUFFET

Made to a design attributed to J.P. Seddon, an architect and advocate of the Gothic style, this massive buffet is almost 8 feet (2.45 m) wide and high. The inlaid and tiled decoration, however, is quite restrained in comparison with some of the heavily carved high-Victorian examples that were made.

The Sheraton style, in which this cabinet was produced, became popular again in the second half of the 19th century. Although many revival pieces were based on 18th-century designs, their proportions and the use of machine-cut veneers indicate a later date of construction.

Bowed hinged doors echo the bow-fronted shape of the top.

"MOUSEMAN" OAK SIDEBOARD

Yorkshireman Robert Thompson, known as the "Mouseman," always signed his work with a small carving of a mouse. Here it is on the left-hand stile. He started making furniture in the 1920s, and craftsmen trained by him are still working today. He believed in traditional methods of hand construction, as the adze-finished top and beaten iron hardware testify.

CABINETS-ON-STANDS

A rectangular structure wih doors behind which are a series of small drawers for storage, the cabinet-on-stand evolved in France and Spain in the early 16th century. These early cabinets were small, often portable, and were usually placed on a table, but later examples were fairly large and had their own matching stands. Such pieces were known in England, but were not made there until after the Restoration in 1660.

Cabinets were designed to hold important papers, coins, or other valuables, and their decoration often reflected this use. In the 17th century, many cabinets were made as diplomatic gifts and might be decorated with a combination of semiprecious stones, gouaches, ivory, panels, gilt-metal mounts, and other materials.

Lacquerware from the East was imported into Europe, where there was a ready market for cabinets which were then fitted with custom-made stands, usually of gilded or silvered wood. The demand for oriental-style furniture also led local cabinetmakers to produce cabinets with japanned decoration to simulate Chinese and Japanese lacquer.

Cabinets-on-stands remained popular pieces of furniture, and in the 19th century many reproductions and pastiches of earlier styles were made.

GEORGE IV SIMULATED ROSEWOOD AND PAINTED CABINET-ON-STAND

Scenes of the Clifton area of Bristol adorn the interior drawer fronts.

Rosewood was popular for furniture making in the early 19th century, and here it has been simulated. Painted decoration was popular in Regency times.

Chinoiserie panel on door. Decoration on cabinets often incorporates oriental motifs.

The legs of stands often get damaged and are repaired or replaced. Check that there are no differences in color and that there is no distressing in areas that are not normally subject to wear and tear.

Panels of flowers alternate with local scenes on the 12 drawers.

Many stands are not original, but this should be obvious from the veneer — the thinner the veneer, the more likely it is to have been machine cut.

The scrolling foliage, imitating ivory inlay, is of Indian inspiration.

The overall shape is typical of both English cabinets of this time and French Empire furniture.

Feet should always show signs of wear.

The painted decoration reflects a love of the exotic, perhaps best witnessed in the design and decoration of Brighton Pavilion.

SPANISH CHESTNUT VARGUEÑO
Popular in 16th- and 17th-century Spain, vargueños are often quite plain on the outside with simple iron or metal decoration, but the built-in interiors are usually highly decorated. There are iron carrying handles on the sides. The stand, although of a later date, is of a traditional form. An original stand is a bonus, but the value of these pieces lies in the cabinet rather than the stand.

FLEMISH MARQUETRY CABINET-ON-STAND
With its silver mounts, carved figures, and inlay, this ornate piece is a good example of the baroque style of cabinet made in 17th-century Europe. The doors open to reveal a built-in architectural interior. Such cabinets were prestigious objects, often given as diplomatic gifts.

WILLIAM III KINGWOOD CABINET-ON-STAND
Although English, this cabinet is of a shape and style that was also popular in Holland and France. The elaborate floral marquetry panels and oyster veneer are typical of the period. In some English variations of this design, there is a convex-fronted drawer in the frieze below the cornice.

DISPLAY CABINETS

In the 17th century, precious objects were stored in display cabinets made with blind doors, which meant that they had to be taken out of the cabinet before they could be seen and admired. This was remedied in the early 18th century with the introduction of cabinets with glazed doors.

Display cabinets come in various shapes and sizes, varying from cabinets-on-stands to corner cupboards and large breakfront pieces with glazed upper doors and cupboards or drawers in the lower section. Many copies, in 18th-century styles, have been made since the late 19th century.

Side cabinets first appeared in the late 18th century. Made in pairs, they were often placed against the piers between windows; those with display shelves above the cabinet are known as chiffoniers. One popular form of side cabinet in the 19th century was the credenza. These D-shaped cabinets with glazed cupboards at each end were often topped by a built-in mirror, although many of them have been removed or lost. Another popular type of display cabinet was the vitrine, often made and decorated in the 18th-century French style, with a bombé or serpentine front, and embellished with ormolu or marquetry.

DUTCH WALNUT AND MARQUETRY BOMBÉ CHINA CABINET

Blind doors can be altered by adding glass panels to make a more saleable object. Check that glazing bars hold individual panes of glass and have not simply been fitted in a decorative pattern to a single large pane. Large glass panes were not made in the 18th century.

The sides should have a stepped joint between the lower and upper sections, and not be in one piece.

The marquetry on this late 18th-century piece is original, but many plainer pieces of furniture have been "enhanced" with floral marquetry to make them more desirable. This should be apparent both from the construction of the piece and from the marquetry itself, which is unlikely to be as well executed as on an authentic 18th-century cabinet.

Ball and claw feet are usual on such cabinets, as are the hairy paw or curved bracket shapes.

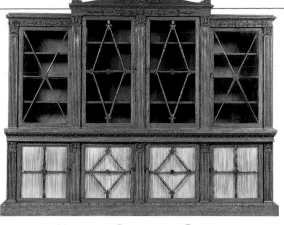

MAHOGANY BREAKFRONT CABINET

The breakfront central section of this cabinet made in the early 19th century has doors incorporating lozenge-shaped glazing bars, while the two side sections have X-shaped bars. The lower section is straight-fronted with doors backed with green silk and, again, the glazing style of the center and side sections differs. The whole stands on an acanthus-carved plinth.

LOUIS XV KINGWOOD MEUBLE D'APPUI

This cabinet has been altered since it was first made so that it now resembles the credenzas and side cabinets popular in 19th-century Britain and France. The central portion is basically period, although glass panels have been added to the doors. The shelved sections at each end are later additions.

MID-GEORGIAN MAHOGANY CHINA CABINET

From the molded cornice downward, the severely rectangular outline of this simple cabinet, repeated in the geometrical pattern of the glazing bars, provides an elegant framework that will not detract from the objects on display inside. The velvet-lined interior is a later alteration.

Carved floral cartouche.

Arched molded cornices on such pieces often held a garniture of Delft vases.

Shelves on 18th-century pieces fit into grooves on the side of the case. If they rest on cleats, they are later additions.

Handles can be a good aid to dating, but are often changed to reflect current taste.

The bombé shape of the lower half, with its convex and concave drawers, was popular in Holland throughout the 18th and 19th centuries. It is found on cabinet bases, armoires, desks, and chests.

CORNER CUPBOARDS

First made in the late 17th century, corner cupboards were often an integral part of the pine paneling of a room and were used to display ornaments such as china or silver. They remained popular throughout the 18th century, although in wealthier households, double-height floor-standing cupboards were increasingly preferred to the hanging variety.

Corner cupboards were made from pine, oak, or walnut or mahogany veneers on a pine carcass. In addition to plain or inlaid wood, some had painted decoration of flowers or an elegant scene; others were japanned. The cupboard doors were either blind or had glazed panels so that the contents could be seen. It was customary to leave blind doors open for the same reason.

The encoignure, a French invention, is a floor-standing corner cupboard often made with a matching chest of drawers. Like many French ideas, it was copied throughout Europe and adopted in England early in the second half of the 18th century. Encoignures were sometimes made with a series of open, graduated shelves above the cupboard, an arrangement that in Victorian times evolved into the corner whatnot.

AMERICAN CHIPPENDALE CORNER CUPBOARD

Interiors sometimes have a semidomed top which is often quite elaborately carved.

Individual panes of glass are used between the glazing bars. Later examples usually have single large panes with molding applied to resemble glazing bars.

Poplar, as here, was a common wood for such cupboards, which were often painted to match the room for which they were made. Old painted surfaces "tone down" over the years and always show signs of wear.

Standing corner cupboards are sometimes put together by combining a glazed-door hanging cupboard and a blind-door cupboard. This should be apparent: check that the method of construction, grain of the wood, and moldings on the doors are the same. Some American cupboards at this time were constructed in a single piece.

Many corner cupboards do not have handles, simply a lock and key. Handles are often replaced — look inside for telltale holes.

The tops and backs of corner cupboards, both freestanding and hanging, are always unfinished. This one was made in the mid-Atlantic states between 1760 and 1780.

A roundel in each corner tops the molded border of the upper section.

Shelves are often nailed in place through the backboards. Some shelves are grooved to allow plates to stand upright; others have applied molding for the same purpose.

Hinges suffer when doors are left open and often have to be replaced. This does not detract from the value of a piece as long as they are sympathetic in style.

Blind paneled doors in the lower cupboard are usual.

The base, here molded, will usually show signs of wear.

MID-18TH CENTURY DUTCH HANGING CORNER CUPBOARD
In rural areas, hanging corner cupboards were common well into the 19th century. This piece is of the popular bow-fronted shape, and its front and angles are painted — a little naively — with flowers, birds, and fruit. Only 35 inches (88 cm) high, it has a plinth base and would originally also have had a molded cornice or superstructure on the top.

GEORGE III MAHOGANY CORNER CUPBOARD
This elegant narrow standing corner cupboard is a classic example of the type that was popular on both sides of the Atlantic and is still reproduced today. The glazing bars on reproductions sit in front of a single pane of glass; 18th-century cupboards have individual panes between the glazing bars.

LOUIS XV KINGWOOD AND MARQUETRY ENCOIGNURE
Stamped BVRB, this encoignure was made by arguably the greatest Louis XV *ébéniste*, Bernard II van Risenburgh. Its curvilinear shape is emphasized in the scrolling purple heart inlay that surrounds the door. The spray of flowers is worked from end-cut marquetry.

CANOPY
The wooden framed covering found over beds supported by four or two posts, also known as a tester. Where it covers only part of the bed, it is known as a half-tester.

CORNICE
The support for bed hangings.

BED HANGINGS
Hangings were usually made of the same fabric as other upholstered pieces in the room; they sometimes also matched the wall hangings.

HEADBOARD
The paneled section at the head of a bed, which also sometimes forms part of the support of a canopy.

END POST
The post found at the foot of a bed.

PILLOW
A cloth case stuffed with feathers used to support the head while asleep.

MATTRESS
A strong cover filled with straw, feathers, or horsehair – and often incorporating springs – to make a flat pad which sits on the webbing or frame.

FRAME
The structural elements of a piece of furniture.

BEDS & BEDROOM FURNITURE

Today's bedrooms are private places in which to sleep and rest, but this has not always been the case. In the 16th and 17th centuries, many houses had interconnecting rooms, so to gain a measure of privacy, curtains around the bed were essential. They also helped to protect the occupants from drafts. As late as the 18th century, the bedroom in grand houses was a focus of daily life: it was customary to receive friends and visitors there and the French kings' habit of holding a reception in the bedroom on rising (*levée*) and going to bed (*coucher*) was copied elsewhere in Europe.

Most bedrooms held a coffer or chest for storage from medieval times on, but other pieces of essential bedroom furniture were introduced in the course of the 18th century. They included a dressing table, linen press or armoire, washstand, and bedside cabinet. Increasingly, and especially from the 19th century on, these pieces were made as a set to match the bed.

OTHER USEFUL TERMS

PILASTER Partial column on the face of a piece of furniture, often rectangular in section.

PLINTH A solid base section used instead of legs on beds and cabinet furniture.

POST An upright support. See COLUMN.

STILE The vertical member of a framework placed at the end or corner of a piece of paneled furniture.

WEBBING The bands of strong material, such as jute, which are interwoven and secured between the frame to support the mattress. Wooden supports may also be used.

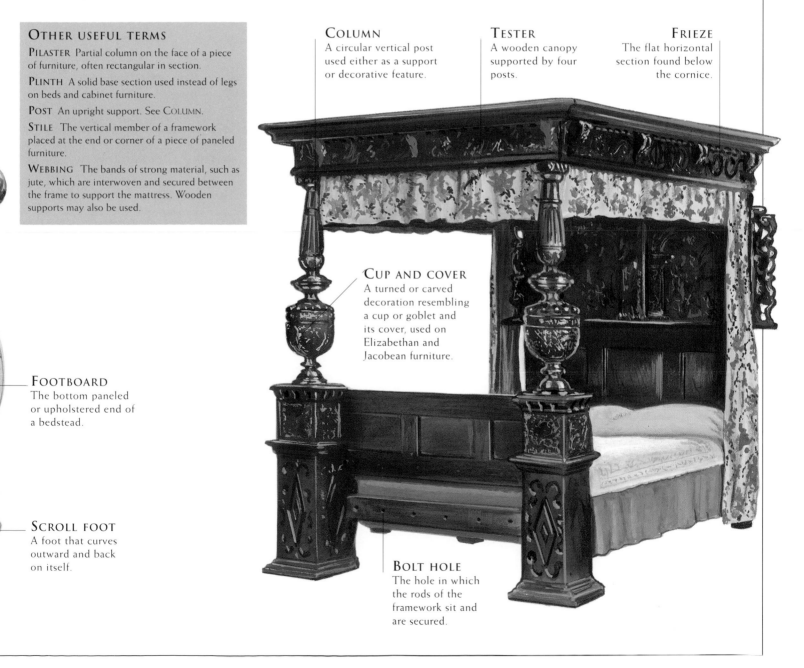

COLUMN
A circular vertical post used either as a support or decorative feature.

TESTER
A wooden canopy supported by four posts.

FRIEZE
The flat horizontal section found below the cornice.

CUP AND COVER
A turned or carved decoration resembling a cup or goblet and its cover, used on Elizabethan and Jacobean furniture.

FOOTBOARD
The bottom paneled or upholstered end of a bedstead.

SCROLL FOOT
A foot that curves outward and back on itself.

BOLT HOLE
The hole in which the rods of the framework sit and are secured.

DESIGN DETAILS

The age of a four-poster bed can often be ascertained from the form and decoration of its front posts, with both overall shape and decorative motifs altering quite subtly over a relatively short period in the 18th and 19th centuries. Although not all 18th-century beds had a canopy, most beds with a footboard and headboard date from the 19th century or later. This includes wooden and upholstered examples, as well as the then innovative brass beds. The Victorians were also not averse to assembling four posters from old wood and paneling.

Some bedroom pieces, including chests and armoires, are covered in other chapters, since the matching bedroom set, in the modern sense, is a 19th-century invention.

Types of bed

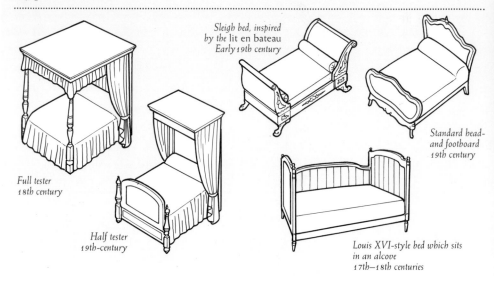

Sleigh bed, inspired by the lit en bateau
Early 19th century

*Standard head-
and footboard
19th century*

*Full tester
18th century*

*Half tester
19th-century*

*Louis XVI-style bed which sits
in an alcove
17th–18th centuries*

Toilet mirrors

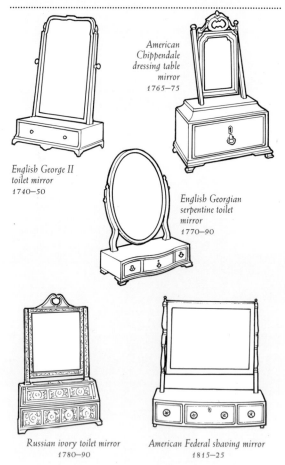

*American
Chippendale
dressing table
mirror
1765–75*

*English George II
toilet mirror
1740–50*

*English Georgian
serpentine toilet
mirror
1770–90*

*Russian ivory toilet mirror
1780–90*

*American Federal shaving mirror
1815–25*

Bedpost styles

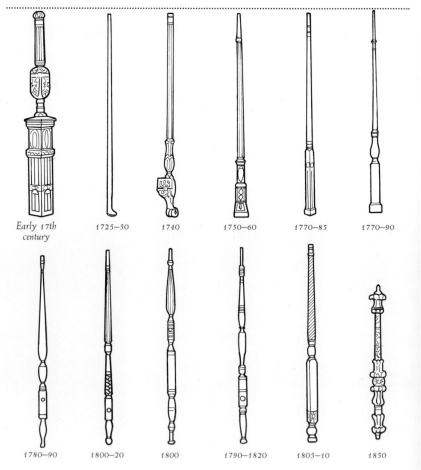

*Early 17th
century*

1725–50

1740

1750–60

1770–85

1770–90

1780–90

1800–20

1800

1790–1820

1805–10

1850

Headboards and footboards

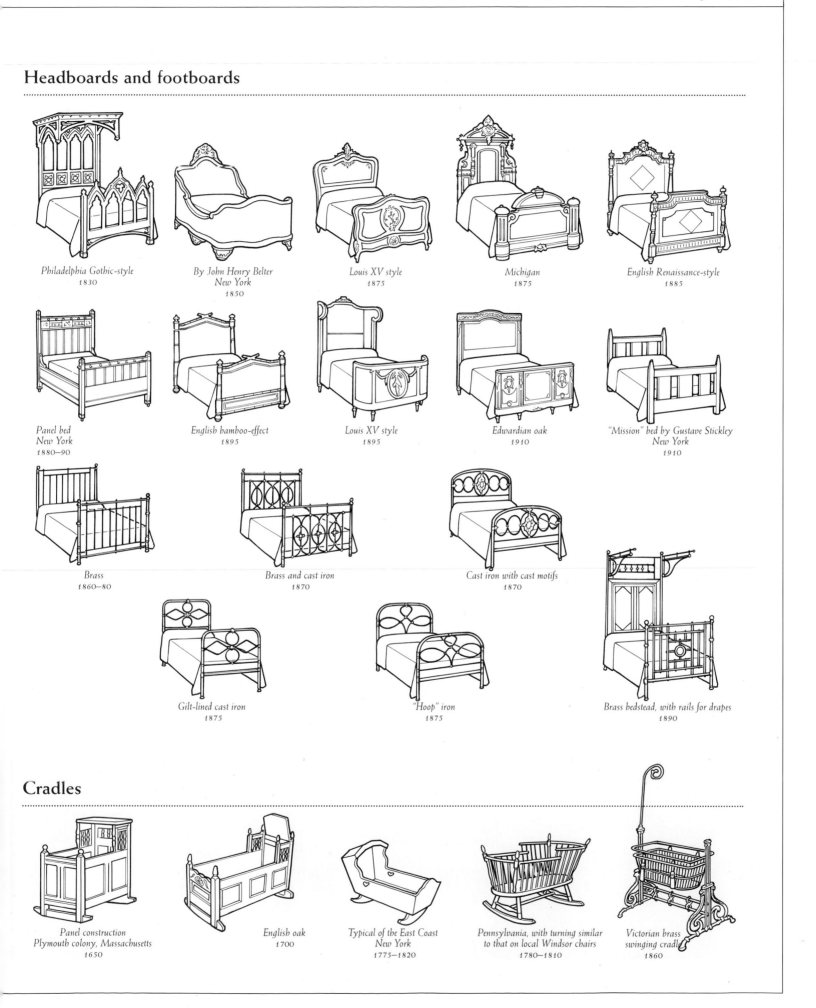

Philadelphia Gothic-style
1830

By John Henry Belter
New York
1850

Louis XV style
1875

Michigan
1875

English Renaissance-style
1885

Panel bed
New York
1880–90

English bamboo-effect
1895

Louis XV style
1895

Edwardian oak
1910

"Mission" bed by Gustave Stickley
New York
1910

Brass
1860–80

Brass and cast iron
1870

Cast iron with cast motifs
1870

Gilt-lined cast iron
1875

"Hoop" iron
1875

Brass bedstead, with rails for drapes
1890

Cradles

Panel construction
Plymouth colony, Massachusetts
1650

English oak
1700

Typical of the East Coast
New York
1775–1820

Pennsylvania, with turning similar
to that on local Windsor chairs
1780–1810

Victorian brass
swinging cradle
1860

CANOPIED AND ENCLOSED BEDS

The late 17th and early 18th centuries were the halcyon days for four-poster, or tester, beds. Examples still exist of these beds, which could be enclosed by their heavy curtains to form a small refuge offering privacy and protection from drafts. From the oak-constructed examples of the 16th and early 17th centuries, four-posters evolved into elaborate manifestations of the upholsterer's art, hung with as costly a material as their owners could afford.

In 18th-century France, a whole variety of four-poster style beds existed, among them the *lit à la polonaise* in which a domed canopy rested on iron supports. It was a style copied elsewhere in Europe, including Regency England. Some beds stood in curtained alcoves; since they stood like a sofa in the alcove and were accessible only from the side that faced into the room, these beds have no canopy.

Not all beds, of course, had testers, and there are European and American examples with short posts or simply a headboard, with or without a footboard. One demand from travelers and military men was for a portable folding bed that could be used on journeys and campaigns. This later found expression in a series of steel or iron beds made in late 18th-century France that were designed, often incorporating neoclassical decoration, for domestic use.

17TH-CENTURY OAK TESTER BED

This bed has a full canopy, or tester. From the second half of the 17th century onward, beds were also made with a half-tester.

Turned columns are usual on early oak testers.

The frieze below the tester at the head of the bed is carved with lunettes and foliage.

The end posts are decorated with a trelliswork of flower heads. Normally only the end posts are decorated on a tester bed as they are the only ones visible when the bed is hung with drapes during the day. Treat four carved posts with suspicion.

Bolts stand away from the wood they secure due to shrinkage.

The stuffed mattress found on these beds was supported by ropes and cords which were slotted through the side rails of the bed. Later, wooden slats were also used

The panels of the tester are carved with lozenges. Sometimes beds are reduced in height (and width) to fit into modern living spaces. Check that decorative carving is continuous.

Carved caryatids flank the headboard's arched panels. These beds were reproduced in the 19th century or made up from old elements, such as panels of wainscoting. When made with genuine old wood, they can be deceptive: check construction method and carving. Victorian carving will be obvious.

The mahogany posts from 18th-century beds were sometimes converted, with relevant additions, into torchères in the early 20th century.

STATE BED

This bed, which dates from about 1715, is thought to have been a royal gift. The Chinese silk hangings – a splendid example of the upholsterer's skill – are original and in excellent condition: the bed, which was too large for any of the family rooms at Calke Abbey, Derbyshire, was in storage for 250 years. Peacock feathers have been used for the tree trunks and butterfly wings.

GEORGE III CREAM- AND BLUE-PAINTED TESTER BED

Dating from the late 18th century, this bed has neoclassically inspired painted decoration along the front and sides of its canopy, and the top is edged with dog-tooth carving. The front posts are later dating from the reign of William IV. The mattress and box spring are, of course, later, too.

WALNUT AND PARCEL-GILT LIT EN BATEAU

Typical of Empire-style beds, this one has drapes suspended from a giltwood eagle and held at the sides by lion masks and rings. Beds of this type always have head- and footboards of the same height. The use of walnut instead of mahogany, combined with the decorative features, indicates that the bed could have been made in northern Europe, probably Germany, during the early 19th century.

OPEN BEDS

Testers were made throughout the 18th century, but declined in popularity during the 19th in favor of half-testers and other styles, among which was the *lit en bateau*. This was popular in the early 19th century, and many examples of its type are found throughout Europe and in America. The introduction of the coiled spring, patented in 1828, meant that a sprung mattress added greatly to the sleeper's comfort.

Reproductions of earlier styles were made alongside new designs. Among the innovations were beds made from metals such as iron and brass, which quickly found favor as they were believed to be healthier than other styles. Such beds ranged from ornate brass designs for the well-off to simple iron bedsteads in humbler homes.

Elaborate bedroom sets were made with beds, armoires, dressing tables, chests,

cabinets, and chairs. They were often of vast proportions and decorated in the latest styles such as Arts and Crafts, Sheraton revival, or Art Nouveau. The market for canopied beds had faded by the beginning of the 20th century, with the familiar higher headboard and lower footboard becoming commonplace.

GEORGE IV GRAY-PAINTED DOUBLE BED

The channeled ogee pediment of the headboard, with its acanthus scrolls, is centered by a viscount's coronet on a tasseled pillow.

In shape and style, the bed could have been made in the middle of the 20th century; construction methods and the Gothic details, however, confirm that it dates from the early 19th.

Box spring and fitted mattress. Many old beds do not have mattresses, and since their sizes are usually different from those of today's beds, mattresses often have to be specially made for them. Take this into account when purchasing a bed — antique beds can appear to be "bargains" without this additional expense.

The paneled frieze with entrelac and patera carving is original to the bed.

The gray painting is not original; there are traces of former gilding on the frame.

The paneled octagonal front posts are topped by domed cupolas, and between them the footboard is decorated with Gothic-shaped panels and a molded top rail. All the decorative devices are mainstream Gothic revival motifs.

In overall appearance, this bed is based on an 1808 George Smith design for a state bed, but it also contains elements from the St. Edward's Chair in London's Westminster Abbey.

The turned finials are a later "improvement."

Octagonal domed feet echo the shape of the cupolas.

FRENCH DOUBLE BEDSTEAD

This kingwood, tulipwood, and marquetry bedstead is in the Louis XV style, which enjoyed a renewed period of popularity in the late 19th century. The gilt-chased bronze mounts echo the floral marquetry of the headboard and footboard. This bed is of high quality, with the headboard beautifully quarter-veneered, and is similar in style to the work of the firm of Zweiner, one of the leading Parisian furniture makers of the time.

BRASS SINGLE BED

Typical of the metal beds made in the 19th century, this was purchased from the London firm of Heals in 1894. Some beds of this type have a half-tester, a canopy that extends over about a quarter of the bed; others have short side wings from which curtains can be hung. Simple brass beds are still made today, and old styles are reproduced.

EMPIRE MAHOGANY BED

Somewhat simpler in style than the *lit en bateau*, this takes its shape from the classically inspired daybeds that had first become popular in the closing years of the 18th century. The ormolu mounts, including Etruscan helmets and the martial trophy on the footboard, reflect contemporary fascination with military campaigns. The castors are later additions.

ARMOIRES

In Europe "armoire" describes a piece of furniture in which linen, clothes, and other household goods are stored. Armoires vary greatly in shape and form; among the more sophisticated city-made examples are those by Boulle and Cressent and the German baroque *schranck*, often decorated with elaborate marquetry and parquetry.

But there are also many country versions which vary from the painted Scandinavian and Germanic pieces to the carved armoires found in most of the provinces of France. Armoires are still made today.

By the end of the 18th century in England, linen presses were being made with flanking cupboards in which to hang clothes. This style remained popular in the 19th century, but from the 1860s onward, "wardrobes" with full-length doors and a central mirror plate were made alongside them. They were often of monumental proportions and formed part of a set of bedroom furniture, usually in one of the many revival styles.

GILLOW AND CO. "STAFFORD" WARDROBE

Walnut and satinwood (for the door panels) are used in the construction of this piece.

Painted decoration was a feature of both Arts and Crafts and Aesthetic style furniture. Here the paneled doors of the central section are painted in oils with scenes representing spring and autumn.

The armoire is typical in both form and size. Two hanging cupboards flank drawers and closed shelves, and it is 8 feet 6 inches (101 cm) wide.

The apron is straight in the center and waved on the flanking cupboards.

Three-quarter spindle gallery with turned corner finials.

The molded cornice is carved with rosettes.

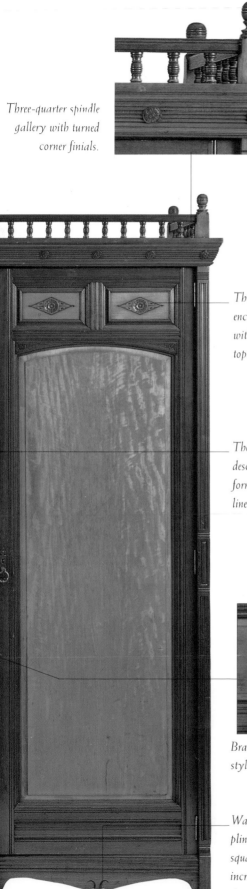

The side cupboards are enclosed by paneled doors with carved lozenges in the top panels of each.

The central section is descended in shape and form from 18th-century linen presses.

Brass handles are stylistically correct.

Wardrobes were still made with plinth bases at this time, although square-section legs, as here, became increasingly common at the end of the 19th century.

LOUIS XVI VERNIS MARTIN ARMOIRE

The doors of this richly decorated armoire by François Duhamel are covered by a gilt-metal trellis with applied paterae. Here the blue-green ground of the decoration – invented by the four Martin brothers in the 1730s, hence the name – is overlaid with polychrome musical and floral trophies. The block-shaped feet are mounted with ormolu lion's paws.

DUTCH WALNUT ARMOIRE

This armoire is of a shape popular in 18th-century Holland; like most Dutch armoires, it is not decorated with marquetry – marquetry on Dutch armoires is usually a sign of later improvements. It has a shaped, molded cornice with a central foliate platform. The interior consists of three sliding shelves, and it stands on bun feet; hairy paw feet are also common on these pieces.

LOUIS XVI ARMOIRE

Constructed in kingwood and tulipwood, with parquetry decoration and ormolu mounts, this armoire was made by Pierre-Harry Mewesen in the 1780s. Below the marble top is a single frieze drawer, which sits above the two paneled doors. The interior is fitted with three shelves. A flaming vase with foliate scrolls is mounted on the drop, and the doors are edged with foliate borders.

DRESSING TABLES

Early dressing tables were cloth-covered side tables on which a small mirror and jars and pots of cosmetics could be stood. Although purpose-made pieces were being produced by the early 18th century, simply draping a table remained a practice well into the 19th century and beyond.

In America, kneehole side tables with an arched frieze and a drawer on each side and a freestanding mirror on top were popular in the 18th century, while in England two types of dressing tables became common. The first was a dressing chest with either a hinged top or a deep built-in top drawer in which there were compartments and a mirror. The other was a table with hinged flaps which opened to the side to reveal a mirror – which could be raised when needed – and built-in compartments on each side. This is similar to the European *poudreuse* or *table à coiffeuse*.

By the early 19th century, pedestal-type dressing tables had evolved. These included a built-in top mirror which was later often flanked by a bank of small drawers. Simpler table examples with frieze drawers were also made throughout the 19th century.

GEORGE II WALNUT KNEEHOLE DRESSING TABLE

Hinges, locks, and escutcheons are correct for the period. If in doubt about replacement drawer hardware, check inside for the telltale holes of the originals.

The mirror is hinged and can be raised on a rack when in use. Mirrors are vulnerable and have often been replaced; since this is so common, it may not affect value.

The breakfronted bow-shaped top is hinged, and the molded edge is typical of pieces made in the 1730s.

Burl and figured walnut have been used in the construction, with both cross- and featherbanding throughout.

The lids cover compartments and wells in which accessories and containers were kept.

The arched central recess has a cupboard at the back and is flanked by two sets of drawers.

The fluted pilasters on the front of the piece are topped by scrolls and acanthus carving.

There is a brass plaque on the other side stating that this dressing table once belonged to Lord Byron. Such attributions tend to make pieces more expensive at auction simply by generating more interest in them.

Two dummy drawer fronts flank a central panel; the built-in interior lies behind them.

AMERICAN WALNUT LOWBOY

This style derives from late 17th-century side tables that could be used either as writing tables or, with the addition of a freestanding mirror, as dressing tables. In America, lowboys were often made in matching sets with a highboy, as is the case with this one, made for the Gilbert family of Salem, Massachusetts, between 1750 and 1770.

TOILETTE À TRANSFORMATIONS

Made in England in about 1910, this tulipwood, marquetry, and parquetry table with ormolu mounts is a copy of one attributed to the 18th-century French cabinetmaker Jean François Leleu. It is a combined writing and dressing table, which opens to reveal a mirrored center drawer with hinged compartment below; there is a drawer on each side, both of which contain additional hinged compartments.

ORMOLU-MOUNTED PORCELAIN AND EBONY DRESSING TABLE

Sèvres or other porcelain plaques are found on 18th-century furniture, but the decoration on the plaques and the overall shape of this Louis XVI-style piece indicate it is not 18th century in origin; it was made in about 1880. The oval mirror's channeled frame is decorated with putti and jeweled plaques, while the top and friezed drawer are painted with scenes of lovers. The table stands on fluted tapering legs.

Plinth base.

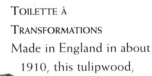

SMALL BEDROOM FURNITURE

Before the introduction of dressing tables, it was usual to place a freestanding mirror on top of the side tables or lowboys used in their place. Known as toilet mirrors, they had a base fitted with drawers in which toiletries could be stored. They were produced throughout the 18th century, even after the introduction of the dressing table, and were often placed on a chest of drawers in a gentleman's bedroom. Full-length mirrors supported on a wooden frame which could be angled to give the best reflection were also common until mirrored armoires appeared in the 19th century. Such mirrors are known as cheval mirrors.

The need for a chamber pot in the bedroom necessitated a piece of furniture in which it could be housed, hence such pieces as the French shelved *table de nuit* and the English cupboard variety. Night tables are found in a variety of styles, reflecting the era in which they were made.

Washing daily did not become fashionable until the mid-18th century, and the earliest washstands date from that time. They are usually tripod shaped, but rectangular ones are also found. More elegant corner washstands first appeared at the end of the 18th century.

PINE CORNER WASHSTAND

The shape of this washstand echoes that of the mahogany corner washstands produced to designs by both Hepplewhite and Sheraton.

Part of a set of furniture made for Dromore Castle in Ireland in the 1860s, this piece was designed by E.W. Godwin and made by William Watt; these attributions add significantly to its value.

Most Victorian washstands have marble tops, and some have marble splashbacks as well. A pitcher and bowl and various other matching articles stood on the top, even when they were not being used.

This washstand has a cupboard in its base in which the chamber pot could be kept. Many of the rectangular Victorian washstands, however, only have a couple of frieze drawers and stand on tapering legs.

The top panels are inset with raffia. When Godwin designed this furniture, he was at a transitional point in his career, between designing in the Gothic style and moving toward the Japanese influences that typify his Aesthetic-style furniture.

Many Victorian washstands, as here, have tiled paneled splashbacks. They vary from decorated tiles to plain green-glazed examples.

The lock plate and handle are electroplated; electroplating became increasingly common after the mid-19th century as an alternative to mercury gilding, a process that resulted in the emission of noxious fumes.

Castors facilitate movement around the room — the weight of marble and tiles makes these pieces heavy.

EMPIRE CHEVAL MIRROR

The basic shape of this ormolu-mounted mahogany mirror, probably made in Germany, was common to many countries, with decoration varying from formal, as here, to painted chinoiserie. Many have adjustable candle arms; here they are scrolled. The brass castors facilitate the mirror's movement. In France such mirrors are also known as Psyche.

QUEEN ANNE WALNUT TOILET MIRROR

This early swing-frame mirror has a typical miniature bureau base with an interior of built-in pigeonholes and drawers that was popular in the early 18th century. Late 18th-century examples often have shield-shaped mirrors and two small drawers in the base.

WALNUT BEDSIDE CUPBOARD

One of a pair, this northern Italian neoclassical-style bedside cupboard was made in the late 18th century. It is crossbanded with tulipwood, and the doors are inlaid with check stringing and, at the center, stars. This one stands on tapering legs, but in the 19th century such cupboards were often made with pedestal bases.

GEORGIAN MAHOGANY WASHSTAND

Dating from the mid-18th century, this tripod washstand is, like many, missing its bowl and pitcher. The bowl fitted into the top, while the pitcher stood on the dished bottom stretcher. The triangular drawer section in between was used for toilet articles. This type of washstand is commonly known as a wigstand, since a wig could be placed in the bowl to be dressed and any powder would be caught in it. Later examples were made in metal.

LIBRARY FURNITURE

The word "library" conjures up a book-lined room furnished with comfortable chairs and sofas and a variety of bookcases, desks, and tables. While such rooms vary widely in style and design details from country to country, the basic furniture necessary to meet the user's needs does not. A place to house books is essential, and bookcases can be either free standing or built-in. Probably next in order of importance is a surface on which to write; this may be a flat-topped writing table, or a desk of some sort. In some cases, these two needs were combined in one piece – the bureau or secretaire bookcase.

Although bookcases and desks are found in most studies and libraries, their use is not restricted to a single room, and many are found in other parts of the house – notably the living room and bedroom – too. Other pieces, however, were designed specifically for use in the library. Among them was a variety of reading tables, on which volumes, plans, and folios could be placed open when needed; and stepladders to allow the library's users to reach the highest shelves. Some of these are instantly recognizable as ladders; others, however, are metamorphic, changing easily from one use to another.

SHELF
The interior of a bookcase may have a series of holes so that shelves can be adjusted.

FRETWORK
Thin pieces of wood cut with a saw into geometric patterns. Fretwork can be open or blind.

CORNICE
Top molding or decorative projection on tall cabinet furniture.

GLASS
Transparent material made from the fusion of silicates, soda, and lime, used in furniture from the late 17th century. Old glass is flat and not as clear as modern glass.

GLAZING BARS
Narrow wooden bars supporting the glass in cabinets.

BREAKFRONT
Protruding center section on a piece of furniture such as a bookcase; a popular style in the 18th and 19th centuries.

BASE
The lower section of large bookcases might contain drawers or shelves.

PLINTH
A solid base section used instead of legs on cabinet furniture.

APRON
Shaped wooden edging below a table top or drawer line.

CYLINDER FALL
Slatted or rigid curved lid that rolls down from within the top of a desk to cover the writing surface.

CABRIOLE LEG
This type of leg was popular in the 18th and 19th centuries.

SABOT
The legs of most French 18th-century pieces end in sabots, to which castors may be attached.

PEDIMENT
Surmounts the cornice in cabinet furniture. Popular forms include swan neck and broken arch.

FALL FRONT
The flap of a bureau or bureau bookcase that pulls forward to provide a writing surface.

BLIND DOOR
A door made completely from wood or another solid material so that the contents of a piece of furniture are not visible when the door is shut; glazed doors, by contrast, allow the interior and contents to be seen when the doors are shut.

PROSPECT DOOR
A door that is carved or decorated to give the illusion of perspective.

PIGEONHOLE
The storage compartments separated by internal divisions found in desks and bureau bookcases.

CONCEALED COMPARTMENT
A drawer in a bureau or cabinet sometimes released by pressing a spring or catch.

DOVETAILS
Machine-cut dovetails are all the same depth; on hand-cut dovetails the depth varies.

DUSTBOARD
The thin piece of wood separating the drawers in a chest, to prevent contents from catching on the drawer above and for security and dust prevention.

BAIL HANDLE
Also known as a drop handle, this was popular in the 18th and 19th centuries.

BOMBÉ
French term for the swollen or bulging shape often used for chests, particularly in continental Europe.

ESCUTCHEON
The shaped plate around a keyhole which helps to protect the wood from damage by the key.

DESIGN DETAILS

The variety of sizes and shapes of library furniture means that there are enormous potential differences between pieces. Moldings, finials, pediments, glazing bars, and interiors are all important factors to look at when considering large bookcases and bureau or secretaire bookcases.

French desks come in a seemingly endless array of sizes, ranging from *bonheurs du jour*, at perhaps 2 feet (60 cm), to roll-top bureaux as much as 6 feet (1.8 m) wide. Some writing tables are supported on legs, others have pedestals fitted with drawers as supports. The various types of desks are illustrated below. The details of the built in interiors of bureau-bookcases also vary enormously.

It is important to remember that the styles of many pieces of library furniture have been copied. But an awareness of what is stylistically correct should make originals and reproductions easy to distinguish.

Glazing

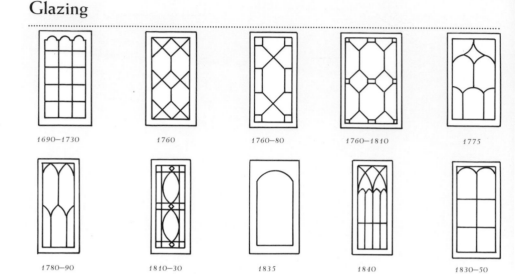

1690–1730   1760   1760–80   1760–1810   1775

1780–90   1810–30   1835   1840   1830–50

Styles and definitions

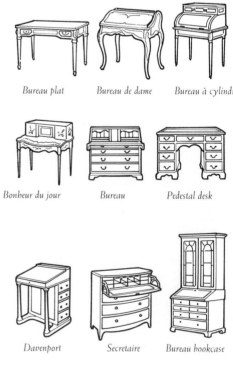

Bureau plat   Bureau de dame   Bureau à cylindre

Bonheur du jour   Bureau   Pedestal desk

Davenport   Secretaire   Bureau bookcase

Desk interiors

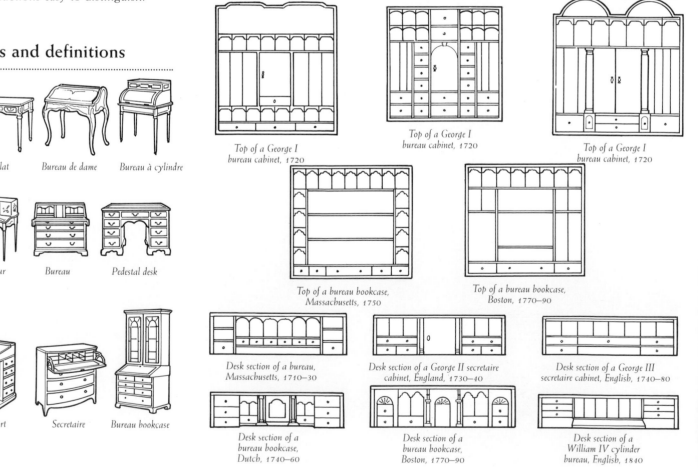

Top of a George I bureau cabinet, 1720

Top of a George I bureau cabinet, 1720

Top of a George I bureau cabinet, 1720

Top of a bureau bookcase, Massachusetts, 1750

Top of a bureau bookcase, Boston, 1770–90

Desk section of a bureau, Massachusetts, 1710–30

Desk section of a George II secretaire cabinet, England, 1730–40

Desk section of a George III secretaire cabinet, English, 1740–80

Desk section of a bureau bookcase, Dutch, 1740–60

Desk section of a bureau bookcase, Boston, 1770–90

Desk section of a William IV cylinder bureau, English, 1840

Moldings, pediments, and finials

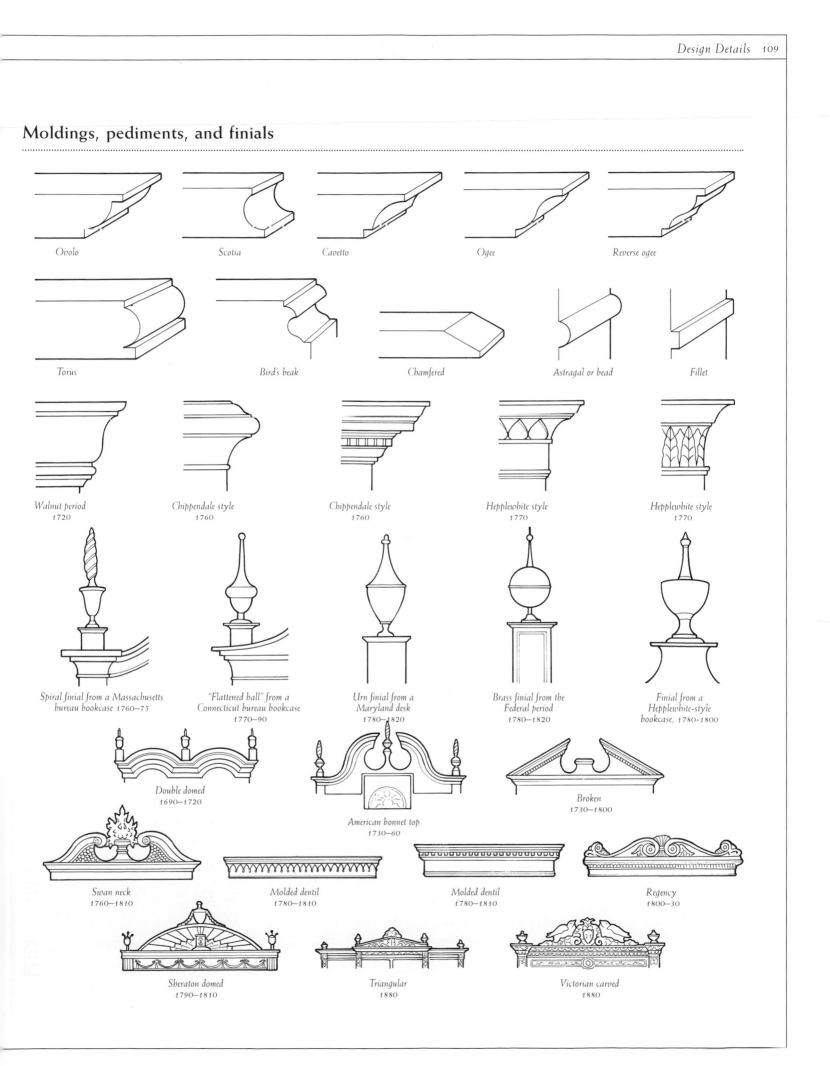

Ovolo

Scotia

Cavetto

Ogee

Reverse ogee

Torus

Bird's beak

Chamfered

Astragal or bead

Fillet

Walnut period
1720

Chippendale style
1760

Chippendale style
1760

Hepplewhite style
1770

Hepplewhite style
1770

Spiral finial from a Massachusetts
bureau bookcase 1760–75

"Flattened ball" from a
Connecticut bureau bookcase
1770–90

Urn finial from a
Maryland desk
1780–1820

Brass finial from the
Federal period
1780–1820

Finial from a
Hepplewhite-style
bookcase, 1780-1800

Double domed
1690–1720

American bonnet top
1730–60

Broken
1730–1800

Swan neck
1760–1810

Molded dentil
1780–1810

Molded dentil
1780–1810

Regency
1800–30

Sheraton domed
1790–1810

Triangular
1880

Victorian carved
1880

BUREAU AND SECRETAIRE BOOKCASES

Among the variations on late 17th-century cabinets-on-stands was one with a fall front which could be used as a writing cabinet. A demand for more storage led to the stand being superseded by a chest, and eventually these pieces evolved to include the three elements that make up a bureau bookcase – a top cabinet, a desk, and a chest base, with the desk and chest base combined in a single piece. Early top cabinets were closed by blind or mirrored doors, but the introduction of glazed doors allowed books inside to be seen. The seam between the two sections was disguised by molding.

Many early 18th-century bureau bookcases are fitted with candle slides at the base of the bookcase section. They can be pulled out and used as stands for candles to provide extra light for the writer at the desk below. This is particularly effective when the doors are mirrored.

Chests-on-chests with secretaire drawers (false drawer fronts that fold down to form the writing surface) were made during the 18th century, but by the second half of the century, they were also being made with a bookcase rather than a chest on top. They became a popular alternative to bureau bookcases with sloping desk tops. Some large bookcases were also fitted with a secretaire drawer.

In Europe, bureau bookcases were regarded as status symbols and were often lavishly decorated, but in France, although there are exceptions, bureau bookcases were not popular.

GEORGE III SATINWOOD AND MAHOGANY SECRETAIRE BOOKCASE

The doors are glazed with rectangular panes, although many bureau bookcases have shaped glazing bars. Check that the glass sits within, rather than behind, the glazing bars.

Crescent-shaped brackets inside the front support the secretaire flap; on bureau bookcases, the writing surface is supported on lopers underneath the flap.

The satinwood interior is fitted with drawers and pigeonholes of various sizes.

The opened flap is lined with leather to form a writing surface.

Tulipwood crossbanding goes across the grain of the veneer.

The top section has a dentilled cornice above the simulated flutes of the frieze. Many bureau bookcases and some secretaire bookcases have a pediment top.

The two shelves are adjustable; this is not uncommon – many bookcases have several grooves to hold shelves.

The two separate sections are often split up and "married" to new partners. Check that the top section is slightly smaller than its base and that molding on the join is the same as that used elsewhere. The top of the lower piece where the bookcase rests should not be veneered. The back edge of the top half should always be flush with that of the bottom half.

Handles, veneers, and any carved decoration should be the same on both sections. The secretaire fall front has applied moldings and handles to resemble two graduated drawers.

Splay feet are typical of late 18th-century bureau bookcases.

QUEEN ANNE WALNUT BUREAU CABINET

The mirrored paneled doors of this crossbanded and feather-strung cabinet open to reveal drawers, pigeonholes (the larger ones could be used to store folios), and cupboards. The columns on each side of the central cupboard are "secret" compartments that can be pulled out. The fall front opens to reveal a similar arrangement of pigeonholes in the desk, and there are candle slides below the cabinet doors.

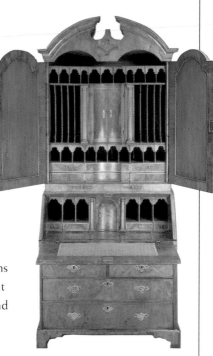

CHIPPENDALE BLOCKFRONT DESK AND BOOKCASE

Made in Massachusetts between 1760 and 1780, this mahogany piece stands on short cabriole legs and ball and claw feet. The fielded paneled doors of the upper section, which is fitted with compartments and pigeonholes, are flanked by columns and surmounted by a dentilled cornice. The interior of the desk is decorated with a fan ornament.

MAHOGANY BREAKFRONT SECRETAIRE BOOKCASE

This is a typical example of a bookcase shape with secretaire drawers. The late 18th-century base, with a central section of drawers – including a secretaire drawer – flanked by cupboards, is topped by bookcases with pierced fretwork glazing bars and crowned by a pagoda-style pediment.

BOOKCASES

Although bookcases from the 17th century and earlier exist, it was not until the beginning of the 18th century that they started to be a more common feature in wealthy households.

In continental Europe, rather more so than in England, bookcases often formed part of the structure of a room, with the result that there are relatively few large 18th-century bookcases in existence; 19th-century "revivals," however, abound. Armoire-style cabinets, used for storing books or other objects, were made, as were low dual-purpose bookcases, known in France as *basses armoires*.

Perhaps the most typical English and American bookcase is the library or breakfront type, in which the central section projects slightly forward of its side wings. Such bookcases have an upper section with glazed doors and a lower section of cupboards enclosed by blind doors. Often very large, bookcases of this type continued to be made into the early 20th century, sometimes in revivals of earlier styles. By the early 19th century, low bookcases and cabinets such as chiffoniers, which could be used in rooms other than the library, were also common.

LATE GEORGIAN SATINWOOD BOOKCASE

As bookcases became popular, some late Georgian and 19th-century breakfront armoires were adapted in this century to "become" 18th-century bookcases. The lower section will have been fitted with blind doors, and the upper with glazed doors as on a bookcase, but the armoire will have been reduced in depth.

Shelves rested on rabbeted grooves in the sides of the upper section of 18th-century bookcases. There should always be enough space above the top shelf to store books.

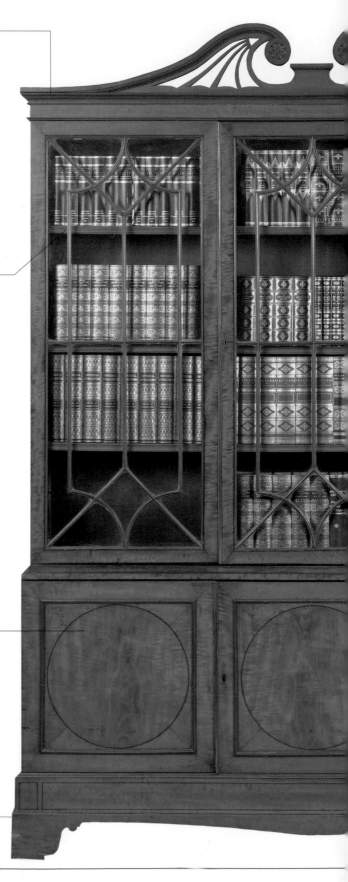

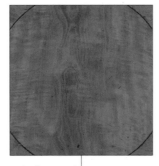

The veneers on the front and sides of all bookcases should always have the same color and grain.

The bracket feet, with their shaped apron, are a later alteration; at this date bookcases either stood on splayed bracket feet or a plinth base. Note the plinth outline above the feet.

The top is centered by a pierced scrolled broken pediment. Large bookcases have sometimes been reduced in size to fit into smaller rooms. In simpler cases, only the pediment may have been removed, but more drastically the carcass may have been reduced in height or width. Telltale signs of an alteration include the proportion of top to base unit: the top should always be appreciably taller than the base.

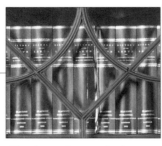

The glazing bars on the doors of the upper section of a period bookcase will be inset to the frame, and usually some of the old thin 18th-century glass panes remain. In the 18th century it was customary to use small panes of glass, even though relatively large sheets were available.

The circular panels of the lower doors are a feature found on many bookcases made at the end of the 18th century.

FRENCH GOTHIC REVIVAL OAK-CANOPIED THRONE

This early 19th-century Gothic revival throne was converted into an open bookcase toward the end of the 19th century – an example of outdated furniture being given a new lease on life. The carving includes such Gothic motifs as angels on the back, arched windows on the pediment, and figures beneath and rosettes and quatrefoils above the arches. The carved panels of the base incorporate fleurs de lis.

LOUIS XV ORMOLU-MOUNTED BIBLIOTHÈQUE BASSE

Richly decorated with end-cut floral marquetry, this kingwood bookcase – one of a pair – is a good example of the small, elegant, but practical furniture found in French private rooms in the 18th century. The block feet with their anthemia mounts are 19th-century English additions.

WALNUT AND EBONIZED BOOKCASE

The firm of Marsh and Jones specialized in Arts and Crafts furniture. This bookcase with a paneled-door base and shelved superstructure is believed to be by Charles Bevan, who designed furniture in the Gothic style for the company. The metal ornamentation is typical of the period.

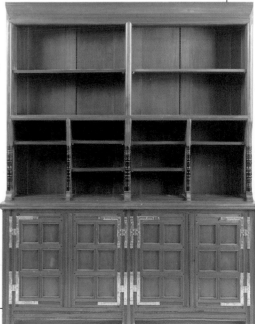

PEDESTAL AND KNEEHOLE DESKS

One of the earliest types of pedestal desk – dating from about 1675 – is the French bureau mazarin. This has a flat rectangular top with a bank of three or four drawers on each side of a central kneehole and stands on eight legs joined by stretchers. The style was copied elsewhere in the late 17th century, but was superseded by the bureau plat early in the 18th century. Some bureaux mazarin were made again in England in the early 19th century when boullework once more became fashionable.

The English version of the pedestal-style desk evolved at the beginning of the 18th century and was designed to stand against a wall. It has a flat rectangular top with a frieze drawer, below which is a recessed central kneehole flanked by drawers; there is usually a cupboard at the back of the kneehole. The relatively small size of these desks has made them popular in the 20th century, and examples have been made up by converting chests of drawers (in fact, these desks developed from the chest of drawers in the first place).

Although kneehole desks continued to be made well into the second half of the 18th century, larger pedestal desks evolved in the middle of the century for use as freestanding pieces of library furniture. Pedestal desks have a rectangular top with three frieze drawers supported by two pedestals, with banks of drawers or cupboards on one side and dummy ones on the reverse; they normally have plinth bases. Some desks were so large that they had drawers on both sides of the pedestals so that two people could use the desk, one sitting on each side; these are known as partners' desks. Desks of this practical type are still used in offices today, and earlier styles have been frequently reproduced.

LOUIS XIV BOULLE BUREAU MAZARIN

The superstructure is an unusual feature, not found on most bureaux mazarins. It contains a central cupboard flanked by drawers.

The handles are typical of furniture of the period.

The leather-lined top has an ormolu border.

Première-partie boullework decorates this desk – the design is cut out in sheets of brass, which are then laid and glued onto sheets of tortoiseshell veneer.

The cabriole legs are an 18th-century alteration: this desk would originally have stood on a leg-and-stretcher arrangement similar to the one on the walnut and ebonized bureau mazarin opposite. Boulle enjoyed a revival in late 18th-century France, and the change may have taken place then. Boullework is highly collectable, so this alteration makes little difference to the desk's value.

Many of these desks are small: some are less than 4 feet (1.2 m) wide.

Boullework (or buhlwork) was a popular form of furniture decoration in the 19th century. Make sure that the brass is in a good state of repair — restoration can prove costly.

Some desks have corner mounts as part of their decoration.

The kneehole is flanked by two sets of three drawers and clearly shows the origins of the pedestal desk.

Hoof feet were used from the late 17th century and throughout the 18th.

WALNUT AND EBONIZED BUREAU MAZARIN
This late 17th-century bureau mazarin has the usual arrangement of eight square tapering legs joined by stretchers, and there is a kneehole cupboard. The name bureau mazarin was coined for desks of this type in the 19th century.

NORTHERN EUROPEAN WALNUT PEDESTAL DESK
This Russian or German desk is decorated with Empire-style ormolu mounts — sea rams and seahorses on the short drawers, griffins on the long drawers, and figures of Victory on the doors. The frieze below the baize-lined top has a long central drawer with a short drawer on each side. These smaller drawers are always the same width as those in the pedestal beneath. Here, paneled doors conceal the drawers within each pedestal.

AMERICAN CHIPPENDALE MAHOGANY KNEEHOLE DESK
Desks of this type, which evolved in England in the early 18th century, were used either as writing tables or, with the addition of a freestanding toilet mirror, as dressing tables. Here, the top drawer is partly fitted, and — as on most such pieces — there is a cupboard at the back of the kneehole. Constructional features and the double-lip molding on the base suggest that the desk was probably made in Norfolk, Virginia.

BUREAUX PLATS

By the beginning of the 18th century, the French kneehole bureau mazarin desk had developed into a form known as a bureau plat – a large, rectangular, flat-topped writing table with frieze drawers. Desks of this type remained popular throughout the 18th and 19th centuries, although they changed in style and decoration to reflect contemporary fashions.

Many bureaux plats were made with a matching freestanding cartonnier (filing cabinet). It is not unusual for cartonniers, which consist of pigeonholes and shelves above a pedestal cupboard, to have become separated from their original bureaux plats.

The fashion in 18th-century France for smaller, more intimate rooms resulted in a demand for smaller pieces of furniture for all purposes, including writing. From the proliferation of small writing tables, in many of which the frieze drawer contained the writing surface, ébénistes in the 1760s produced a new type of writing table with a cabinet superstructure containing drawers or a combination of pigeonholes and drawers. The fitted frieze drawer continued to contain the writing surface, and there was often also an undertier. Known as a bonheur du jour, this type of desk soon found favor elsewhere in Europe.

Writing tables of all sizes, sometimes influenced by French models, were popular in England in the second half of the 18th century. In the 1790s, a model with a D-shaped superstructure evolved. It was known as a Carlton House desk since the Prince of Wales had one in his London home of that name. There is, however, no evidence that the first one was made for him.

LOUIS XVI AMARANTH BUREAU PLAT

The top is inset with green morocco leather edged in gilt tooling in a key pattern with alternating lyres and putti motifs.

Acanthus decoration adorns the corner angles.

The left-hand drawer is stamped J.F. LELEU JME, indicating that the bureau was made by Jean-François Leleu, who produced some of the earliest examples of French furniture in the neoclassical style for the Prince de Condé between 1772 and 1777.

The fluted legs with their crisply cast ormolu capitals and the foliate plaques on the blocks at the top are all hallmarks of the neoclassical style.

The ormolu mounts are of the highest quality.

The green stain of the wood can be seen beneath the ormolu entrelac design of the frieze, which has foliate bosses interspersed with pierced flower heads surrounded by laurel leaves Some of these form the handles of the three drawers.

Steel framing and bolts secure the legs firmly to the frame of the top. Such underpinning is unusual, and is Leleu's solution to a common problem with large bureaux plats — bowing toward the middle. This desk is 6 feet (1.8 m) wide and entirely flat.

EMPIRE-STYLE SATINWOOD BUREAU PLAT AND CARTONNIER

Made late in the 19th century, this ormolu-mounted desk has at one end a cartonnier with open shelves which is surmounted by a clock. In the 18th century, cartonniers were either integral, as here, or stood on a desk's edge or on a separate stand at one end of the desk. They were always designed and made with the desk.

FLEMISH SECRETAIRE CABINET

Made in about 1700, this pewter and brass-inlaid cabinet with a raised superstructure of drawers is a stylistic predecessor of a *bonheur du jour*, but at 35 inches (89 cm), it is wider — most 18th-century *bonheurs du jour* were about 24 inches (60 cm) wide. The elaborate panels depict Europeans in China.

Slides are fitted at each end of some bureaux plats (although not this example); they can be pulled out to provide additional space for writing, documents, or books.

Stepped block feet are typical of the neoclassical style.

GEORGE III SATINWOOD CARLTON HOUSE DESK

These quite large writing tables have frequently been reproduced since the late 19th century. The D-shaped superstructure, here rectangular, is more often curved, as are the drawers.

WRITING DESKS

Found throughout Europe and in America, writing desks are common and developed from the sloping-top writing boxes of the late 16th century. The type is typically a desk that has a writing slope above a chestlike section of drawers which stands, depending on the number of drawers, on legs or bracket feet.

These writing desks were made in England from the beginning of the 18th century, when better-quality pieces were veneered with walnut, but by the 1730s mahogany was the preferred wood. The standard form – a sloping writing flap, which opens to reveal a fitted interior, with a lower drawer section on bracket feet – has altered only in decorative details since then. Both early walnut and Georgian mahogany desks have been much copied in the 20th century, and period pieces have also been "improved" by the addition of inlay or by veneering period oak desks with more expensive wood veneers.

GEORGE II FIGURED WALNUT DESK

The two tiers of the hinged section contain pigeonholes with sliding covers to stop the contents from falling out when the desk is opened or shut.

A fitted interior is a feature of all such desks; this one has a series of drawers flanked by pigeonholes.

One door encloses three drawers, the other folio slides.

Locks and escutcheons are stylistically correct.

Bracket feet are usual on desks of this date, although these are later examples. Earlier desks had bun feet, which were often replaced with bracket feet in the 18th century. Replacement bracket feet are now often changed back to bun feet.

The writing surface can be slid forward when the desk is in use.

The back of most of these desks designed to stand against the wall is not veneered. Those designed to be freestanding usually have a veneered back.

The hinged flap of this desk is unusual; when it is opened, it folds backward to rest on the desk's top, rather than the more usual arrangement of a sloping front that folds outward to rest on lopers.

The joint between the two separate sections of early desks was masked by molding. Even after they were made as one piece, the molding was used as a decorative device until the 1730s.

Carrying handles are usual on early desks. They are particularly appropriate here as this desk belonged to a mid-18th-century admiral and is believed to have gone to sea with him. Other examples of this shape are known.

Featherbanding is widely used as a decorative feature on this desk.

LOUIS XVI TABLE À TRANSFORMATIONS
This small rectangular mahogany and yew table could be taken for a piece of English cabinetmaking at first glance. But the inlaid legs and ormolu drapery mounts indicate that it is not. Some French *ébénistes*, however, did make furniture in "le gout anglais" (to the English taste). The top folds open to form a writing surface, and the superstructure rises on springs to reveal a nest of drawers and pigeonholes.

AMERICAN CHIPPENDALE MAHOGANY DESK
Attributed to John Townsend, one of the most renowned 18th-century cabinetmakers from Newport, this desk has a slant front that opens to reveal a fitted interior with eight valance drawers above the pigeonholes, and drawers and compartments below.

OAK DESK
An exponent of the Arts and Crafts movement, architect Sidney Barnsley not only designed, but also made furniture after 1903. Like this piece, all his furniture was simple and without ornament, dominated by the beauty of the wood and the skill of the maker. The paneled flap encloses a fitted interior, the apron is arched, and the desk stands on molded trestle-type feet.

WRITING DESKS AND SECRETAIRES

The English-style writing desk with a fall front above a series of drawers did not find favor in France, where a slightly different version was produced. It has the same triangular-shaped top section and sometimes one or more frieze drawers but stood on legs. Known as a *secrétaire en pente* (also *bureau de dame* and *bureau en dos d'âne*), this type of desk varied in width from 22 inches (55 cm) to 44 inches (112 cm) and was made from the 18th century onward.

Cylinder or roll-top desks developed in France from *secrétaires en pente*. They have a

writing table base topped by drawers and shelves over which a curved cover can be rolled backward or forward. There are two types of top: the tambour, in which slats of wood, glued to either linen or canvas, roll back like a shutter; and the solid "cylinder" that rolls back into the carcass of the desk between the back of the drawers and the back of the desk. The writing surface slides forward as part of the opening mechanism or has to be pulled forward manually.

French *secrétaires à abattant* evolved from writing cabinets-on-stand. They are

rectangular desks in two parts: a top with a large fall front that opens to form a writing surface and reveal drawers and pigeonholes; and (usually) a lower section of cupboard doors behind which are shelves or drawers. Their large surfaces provided an opportunity for elaborate marquetry decoration or the use of lacquer panels, although later in the century veneers became more common. Popular in France and elsewhere in Europe, where they were used in the more private rooms of the house such as a study, these pieces were in less demand in England.

GERMAN BRASS-INLAID SECRÉTAIRE À ABATTANT

Galleried D-shaped top with the gallery rail echoed in the display shelves.

The top frieze consists of a central drawer flanked by two simulated panel drawers.

The interior shelves and drawers are veneered with Karelian birch, an indication that this desk may have been part of a set of furniture David Roentgen made for Catherine the Great.

The overall shape is based on one that had become popular in France during the 1770s. Some French versions are decorated with Sèvres porcelain plaques on the fall front and the central drawer front.

The shaped and galleried shelves on each side of the fall front were used to display porcelain or other ornaments.

The central drawer is flanked by spring-loaded drawers, opened by releasing a spring catch.

Ormolu mounts vary enormously in quality: these are almost sculptural. Mounts are also lost or replaced, and in the 19th century many were added to pieces to "enhance" them. This is usually obvious: they are less finely cast than period ones, tend to be overelaborate, and do not "sit" well.

...liate spray ...bove putto motif.

The square tapering legs are decorated with milles raies panels and end in block sabots; the toupie capitals are later additions.

LOUIS XV ORMOLU-MOUNTED PARQUETRY BUREAU DE DAME

With its cabriole legs and bombé shape, this small desk is a good example of Louis XV period cabinetwork. The fitted interior is decorated with floral marquetry. This style and shape have been much copied since the 19th century, although materials and construction methods usually make copies evident.

AMARANTH AND MARQUETRY BUREAU DE DAME

This is a German interpretation of French designs by the renowned father and son team, Abraham and David Roentgen. The floral marquetry with its trailing scrolls is typical of their work, as is the fact that the legs are not an integral part – their join to the carcass is concealed by the mounts.

GEORGE III CYLINDER DESK

Attributed to Ince and Mayhew, this English desk dates from 1775 and is decorated with neoclassical marquetry. Check that a desk's cylinder top is in full working order. Both tambours and solid cylinders are vulnerable, and repairs are costly.

The rectangular fall front is centered by a circular panel enclosing a medallion of a putto surrounded by books, to represent learning. The use of a single panel of fine mahogany veneer on the fall front, together with the restrained use of ornament, adds to the evidence that David Roentgen (working in the neoclassical style) may be the desk's creator.

OTHER LIBRARY PIECES

In addition to large writing tables and bookcases, 18th- and 19th-century libraries and studies contained several other pieces of furniture frequently used in the pursuit of business and leisure activities.

The top shelves in both built-in and freestanding bookcases were often out of the user's reach, so library steps were needed. These ranged from large ladderlike structures to pieces of metamorphic furniture such as chairs and tables which could be converted into steps.

Large folios and ledgers needed special tables on which they could be displayed and studied; the architect's table is one such type of table. It had a hinged top that could be raised to hold a book or plans and a front section that, when pulled forward, revealed a writing surface. Smaller reading tables were also made.

Tables known today as drum tables – and widely reproduced, although in smaller dimensions – were also used as writing tables. These are pedestal tables with a drum-shaped top on a pillar support and splayed legs; they also feature drawers and, often, dummy drawers in the frieze.

The davenport is a late 18th-century writing table or desk, characterized by a sloping top above a series of real and dummy drawers and so-called because the earliest recorded example was made for a Captain Davenport by Gillows. Their small size made davenports popular, and they were produced in a variety of styles throughout the 19th century.

GEORGE IV POLLARD OAK DAVENPORT

The leather-lined writing slope slides forward to provide knee space for the writer. The interior below the slope is fitted. Some later davenports have piano-shaped fronts.

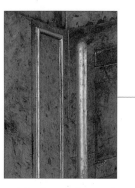

The front is decorated with brass molding.

Simple turned handles are common; brass handles are also found.

Many davenports have similar feet to the compressed bun-type found here. Some also have castors to facilitate movement.

The top has a three-quarter pierced brass gallery. On some later examples, the top has a rising compartment with stationery racks or pigeonholes and drawers; on others, the top is lidded and opens to reveal inkwells and space for pens and nibs.

This small drawer would have held ink and pens.

This example has a slide on each side of the pedestal above the drawers.

Only one set of drawers is genuine; those on the other side are dummy – a regular feature of this type of desk. Some davenports have drawers at the front; in such cases the top usually swivels to one side when needed for use.

This davenport is of pollard oak, which is not unusual, although they occur in many different woods and in such materials as papier mâché.

The lines of this desk are restrained, but by the Victorian age, davenports were being made with either columnar or cabriole legs.

SET OF WILLIAM IV LIBRARY STEPS

Obviously made for a large library, these steps are more than 8 feet (2.4 m) high. The cross-railing at the top is decorated with flower heads, and the rails end in C-scroll supports. The steps rest on four column supports which rise from the rectangular plinth base. These steps are practically a small staircase, but many smaller examples, including folding ones, exist. Library steps were first-made in the mid-18th century and continued to be made throughout the 19th.

GEORGE III MAHOGANY RENT TABLE

A variation of drum tables, rent tables normally stand on square paneled bases, which usually also incorporate a cupboard. Here the 12 frieze drawers are alphabetically "numbered" and once housed the records of tenants' payments. The central well in the top of the table held pens and ink.

GEORGE III ARCHITECT'S TABLE

The hinged top of this mahogany table is raised by a rack and the ledge at the bottom is used to support books. The front section is pulled forward to reveal the baize-lined slide with compartments, including a secret one below. A common feature, the inner columned legs provide extra stability.

STILE
Vertical member of a framework placed at the end or corner of a piece of paneled furniture.

FIELDED PANEL
A flat panel with beveled edges fitting into grooves in the framing rail without glue, to allow the wood to swell or shrink.

MUNTIN
The vertical framework between panels.

MOLDING
A shaped decorative piece of wood applied to furniture, sometimes used to hide joints.

CORNICE
The moulded projection crowning the top of a piece such as a cupboard or hutch. Less elaborate on country pieces than on more upmarket furniture.

GLAZED DOOR
A door wholly or partially made of glass so that the contents of a piece of furniture are visible.

BACKBOARD
One or more pieces of wood joined to form the back of a piece of case furniture. Often painted in hutches.

HUTCH
A piece of furniture consisting of a series of shelves above a cupboard base. There are enormous regional variations in style.

SHELF
On country pieces shelves may have rebates or runners to hold plates upright for display.

PROVINCIAL & COUNTRY FURNITURE

One of the most important factors to remember when considering provincial and country furniture is that while much of it is simple, it is not necessarily crude. In addition, many pieces are traditional to a region, but interpretations of more mainstream styles were also made.

Much country furniture has an enduring appeal – Windsor chairs and hutches, for example, have been made for generations, as have French provincial armoires. And Shaker furniture has been admired since it was first made, so much so that the Shakers were selling it by mail order as early as the late 19th century. But a burgeoning interest in the past has made country furniture particularly popular with collectors today, and as a result the field is broadening. Collectibles now include kitchen equipment as well as furniture. Many kitchen tables, chairs, and hutches were made of pine, which was readily available on both sides of the Atlantic. Such pieces were often painted, although they may have been stripped.

WOOD
A wide variety of woods is used for provincial and country furniture, since readily available local ones are usually preferred. See also pp. 11 and 127.

UNDERSIDE
The underside of table tops will be worn where hands have lifted the table to move it.

BOARDS
The boards used on 16th and 17th-century table tops will have shrunk across the width.

FRIEZE DRAWERS
Most kitchen tables had one or more drawers in the frieze. Handles are often turned.

CLAMPED TOP
A piece of wood with the grain running at right angles to the grain of the planks of a trestle or refectory table.

TURNING
A process whereby wood is shaped on a lathe to produce a decorative effect. See pp. 126–27.

LEGS AND FEET
Country furniture, in particular, stood on stone floors that were frequently washed, so feet and the bottom of legs, here turned, are especially subject to wear.

OTHER USEFUL TERMS
BENDS The curved runners on a rocking chair.

FINIAL Decorative ornament used to finish a vertical structural element.

LADDERBACK Chair with a back consisting of a series of horizontal bars between the vertical uprights, in the manner of a ladder.

PLINTH A solid base section used instead of legs on cabinet furniture.

TRIDARN Welsh dresser made as a small cupboard and display shelves above a press cupboard.

SMOKER'S CHAIR
Chair in which the back rail is continuous with the arms.

DESIGN DETAILS

One of the most important features of country furniture is the use of local woods. Wood should always have acquired the patina of age and show signs of use in places subject to wear. A second feature of country furniture is that many pieces also incorporate purely local features: the racks of hutches made in Yorkshire, for example, incorporate a clock at the center.

Much country furniture was made by traditional means, including joined construction. Carved or painted decoration is usually good, but naive in comparison with more sophisticaed pieces. There are also differences in decorative techniques, such as turning, from region to region. While some country furniture incorporates details taken from contemporary upscale pieces, much does not: makers and buyers preferred to cling to what they knew and what had proved serviceable in the past.

Windsor chairs

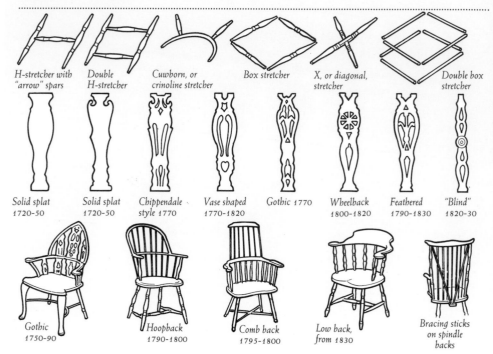

H-stretcher with "arrow" spars

Double H-stretcher

Cwborn, or crinoline stretcher

Box stretcher

X, or diagonal, stretcher

Double box stretcher

Solid splat 1720-50

Solid splat 1720-50

Chippendale style 1770

Vase shaped 1770-1820

Gothic 1770

Wheelback 1800-1820

Feathered 1790-1830

"Blind" 1820-30

Gothic 1750-90

Hoopback 1790-1800

Comb back 1795-1800

Low back, from 1830

Bracing sticks on spindle backs

Styles of turning

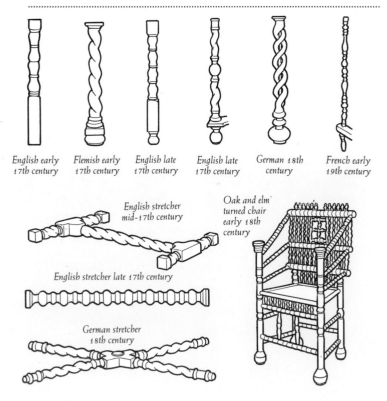

English early 17th century

Flemish early 17th century

English late 17th century

English late 17th century

German 18th century

French early 19th century

English stretcher mid-17th century

English stretcher late 17th century

German stretcher 18th century

Oak and elm turned chair early 18th century

Shaker chairs

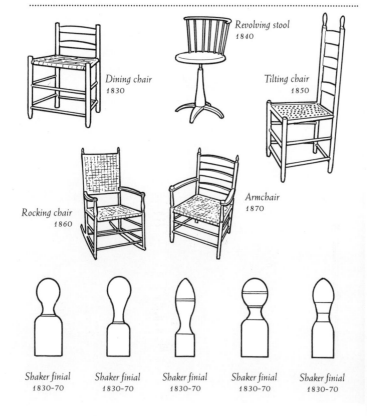

Dining chair 1830

Revolving stool 1840

Tilting chair 1850

Rocking chair 1860

Armchair 1870

Shaker finial 1830-70

Shaker finial 1830-70

Shaker finial 1830-70

Shaker finial 1830-70

Shaker finial 1830-70

Woods

Elm

Cherry

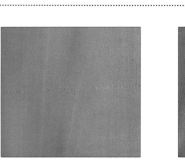

Pear

Yew

Oak

Walnut

Walnut with ash crossbanding

Pine

Hutches

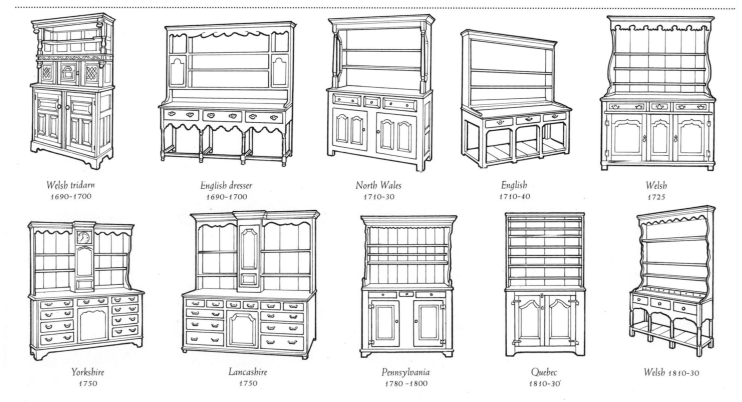

Welsh tridarn
1690–1700

English dresser
1690–1700

North Wales
1710-30

English
1710-40

Welsh
1725

Yorkshire
1750

Lancashire
1750

Pennsylvania
1780 –1800

Quebec
1810-30

Welsh 1810-30

COUNTRY PIECES

Any piece of furniture not made "in town" by a highly trained cabinetmaker, but perhaps by a local carpenter can be described as a country piece. Country furniture is always made from local woods, such as pine, in both Europe and America. Much of it is of traditional design and can incorporate detailing that has been used locally for centuries. The best country furniture is often a simplified interpretation of the designs of some of the leading cabinetmakers of the day.

The exception to this is the settle, which has been made for almost 1,000 years and has always been a purely country piece. Settles with both high and low backs have been produced, as have pieces with more than one use – a settle with a hinged seat for storage, for example, or a hinged back that folds down to rest on the arms and form a table. But chairs, tables, chests, and almost every other piece of furniture were made and used in both town and country.

Reduced versions of current styles were often made for children. Of such furniture, cradles and chairs have survived in the largest quantities.

ENGLISH MAHOGANY CRADLE

The rectangular style of crib that is still used today evolved from the trestle-supported cradle shape and was first introduced in the 19th century.

This cradle has a stylized sunflower carved on the back of the head, which confirms its late 19th-century origin: the sunflower motif was extensively used by the architect and designer Sir Alfred Waterhouse.

The paneled body is very similar to the oak cradles made in the late 17th and early 18th centuries, but the use of mahogany suggests a later date.

Arched hoods are more common [on] 18th-century cradles than th[ose] produced earlier; flattish top[s were] common in the 17th century.

Trestle supports were introduced in the 18th century to prevent animals, such as rats, from getting into the cradle and harming the infant. However, the earlier style, in which the cradle stood on rockers, was still made.

The plain sides indicate an 18th-century or later date of manufacture. Often, 17th-century cradles have some chip-carved decoration, although many carved dates are not original.

Most cradles are quite deep to hold the mattress and several layers of bedclothes.

Many cradles have finials either at the foot, as here, or on the hood, or on all four corners. On cradles with runners, the finial was pushed to rock the baby.

The cradle is suspended from the endpost by a metal "string" so that it can be rocked easily.

The corner supports to which the side panels are attached are square cut.

The base of the cradle might be boarded but was sometimes, like that of a bed, made of webbing or laths.

OAK CHILD'S CHAIR
The paneled back with its carved lozenge, scrolled arms on baluster supports, and turned legs are all typical features of country chairs made during the reign of Charles II. However, its high legs and small size identify it as a child's highchair. The back would originally have had finials.

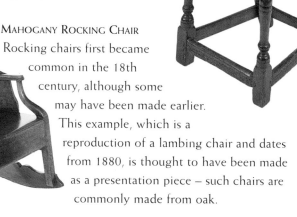

MAHOGANY ROCKING CHAIR
Rocking chairs first became common in the 18th century, although some may have been made earlier. This example, which is a reproduction of a lambing chair and dates from 1880, is thought to have been made as a presentation piece – such chairs are commonly made from oak.

CARVED OAK SIDE TABLE
This provincial side table was made in the 1770s, but has subsequently been improved with the addition of the serpentine apron and carving. Such alterations often detract from the value, but this has been done sympathetically, and the table is worth more than if it had been a simple Georgian piece.

LINCOLNSHIRE PINE DRESSING TABLE
Here a six-drawer chest-of-drawers base has been surmounted by a plain rectangular mirror which is supported by stands decorated with turned bull's-eyes, each of which has a small drawer in its base; the chamfered edges give the piece a little more character than if they had been left plain. This piece was made in about 1880, and its handles are not original.

WINDSOR CHAIRS

Local traditions and craftsmanship are most apparent in country chairs, in which style and decoration are particular to the area where the piece was made. An exception to this is the Windsor chair, since variations on the basic design are found in different regions of England and North America. But, like country chairs, Windsor chairs are always made of local woods.

The earliest Windsor chair shape is the comb back, which has spindle uprights supporting a comb-shaped cross rail at the top. Later examples are known as hoop backs and have a continuous curving rail which rises from the seat. These chairs were reserved for the outdoors by the well-to-do, but in the country they were used by all, both for household purposes and in taverns and other public places. Windsor chairs are still produced to traditional styles in some areas: they have, for example, been made continuously around High Wycombe in Buckinghamshire, England, since the 18th century, although production has been mechanized for the last 100 years.

Other popular types of country chair include the ladderback, which has a back with horizontal slats, hence the name, and the spindle back which has turned uprights. Many country chairs of both types have rush seats. The Arts and Crafts movement spawned a type of spindle-back chair based on traditional designs that was widely copied in the second half of the 19th century.

CHILD'S HOOP-BACK WINDSOR CHAIR

This chair, which dates from about 1850, is made from a combination of yew and beech. Examples that incorporate yew are the most highly sought.

The horizontal bowed rail joining the arms of a Windsor chair is known as a yoke rail. Not all Windsor chairs have high backs; smoker's chairs, have low backs that end at the yoke rail.

The saddle-shaped seat is a usual feature of such chairs. The grain of the wood should be visible on both the seat and its underside.

Every detail on the chair is exactly as it would be on a Windsor chair for an adult, and the overall proportions are correct.

The crinoline stretcher was first used on 18th-century chairs. It is also sometimes referred to as a cowhorn stretcher.

Splats on Windsor chairs come in a variety of shapes, including wheelback, Prince of Wales feathers, and assorted ornate patterns, such as this one.

Heavy turning on the legs indicates a relatively late date of manufacture – the turning on earlier chairs tends to be finer.

YEW AND ELM WINDSOR CHAIR

This 18th-century chair is a good example of the popular Gothic style. The arch-shaped back and the pierced back splats are all in the Gothic taste, as are the pierced ear pieces of the cabriole legs. The seat is elegantly shaped and sweeps inward behind the front legs.

AMERICAN COMB-BACK WINDSOR CHAIR

The serpentine crest rail of this chair made in New England in about 1800 ends in a scrolling ear design, and the armrests end in out-scrolling hand grips. The turned tapering legs are joined by an H-shaped baluster stretcher.

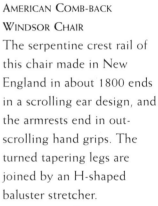

TURNER'S CHAIR

The triangular shape and overall form of this chair can be traced back to the beginning of the 17th century. Sometimes known as "thrown" chairs from the former name for turning, such chairs are masterpieces of the turner's art. This is a 19th-century revival piece.

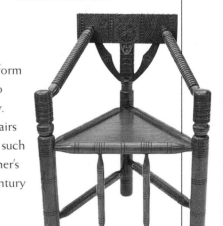

CONTINUOUS ARMCHAIR

The molded crest rail on this chair, made in the 1790s, continues down to form the arms, hence the name. The seat, described as plank, is of typical solid construction and the chair stands on turned tapering legs joined by turned H-stretchers.

SIDEBOARDS AND HUTCHES

One of the most popular and practical pieces of country furniture is still produced today. The hutch, or dresser, which consists of a plate rack above a set of cupboards, evolved in the early 18th century.

Low hutches, which descended from the medieval side tables used for "dressing" meat, were first made in the 17th century. These have three frieze drawers below the rectangular top and stand on turned legs at the front and square legs at the back. By the early 18th century, they were being made with a set of hanging shelves which eventually was made as an integral part. There are many regional varieties in Britain, France – where hutches were always purely provincial pieces – and other European countries. Settlers in America made hutches in their native styles.

The introduction of the sideboard meant that the hutch was relegated to the kitchens of wealthy households, but it remained an important piece of furniture in rural areas. The Arts and Crafts movement's advocacy of traditional skills and furniture forms led to the hutch's renaissance wherever its adherents' ideas prevailed.

MID-GEORGIAN SHROPSHIRE
OAK "DRESSER"

Some hutch racks do not have backboards; in some cases they have been added at a later da

Here the backboards are original, a common feature on hutches made in the northern counties of England.

Hutches are sometimes altered in size to fit into smaller rooms. Look for reductions in the height and width of the rack: the proportions of an altered piece will be wrong. Most bases, as here, are three drawers wide.

Mahogany crossbanding and fluted pilasters are repeated on both top and lower sections.

This hutch stands on ogee bracket feet, although many 18th- and 19th-century pieces of this type have cabriole legs at the front; the back legs are always plain.

Not all hutches have cupboard bases; some have bases similar to chests.

The pierced waved frieze is a pleasing decorative detail, echoed in the aprons of the three shelves.

Dentil molding on the cornice.

Paneled doors inlaid with checked banding enclose two small drawers.

Racks were often added to low pieces at a later date, so check that the wood and any decorative details on the upper and lower sections match.

Period hutches will have had lots of wear, so there should be scratches both inside and out, as well as accumulated dirt and grease in nooks and crannies and around the handles of the drawers and cupboards.

Cupboards in the base are typical on hutches made in northern England.

WELSH DRESSER

Dating from the 1830s, this oak hutch is a fine example of those made in northern Wales. The ivory kite-shaped escutcheons, the simple molding on the cornice, and the geometric colored wood inlays are all typical; and the backboard of the upper section is painted in the traditional manner.

ARTS AND CRAFTS STYLE HUTCH

This piece shows how the Arts and Crafts movement in Britain and the United States sought to go back to simple, traditional styles. Its advocacy of the hutch form, however, meant that hutches were also made in the revival styles popular in the late 19th and early 20th centuries.

KITCHEN FURNITURE

In the high-tech modern world, it is sometimes difficult to imagine the work traditionally involved in running a kitchen. The mistress of the house, whether she had servants or not, was responsible for managing and feeding her entire household. Meats and other provisions had to be prepared and stored for the winter months when fresh produce was scarce. Most 18th-century country households were self-sufficient. The image of a cozy kitchen developed in the late 19th century; before then, the emphasis was on efficiency, with space found only for furniture and utensils that were strictly necessary.

The kitchen table was probably the most important piece of furniture and usually dominated the center of the room. Since the table was also used for dining, most kitchens had either chairs, stools, or even benches. Many kitchens also had a hutch, dough bin, cupboards, and smaller tables. A great deal of kitchen furniture was made from local woods, and much was originally painted. The popularity of stripped pine since the 1960s has meant that many fine pine pieces have now lost their original painted finishes.

In addition to furniture, kitchens were also stocked with the many utensils and equipment used for preparing and cooking food, such as spits for roasting meat, molds, and copper pans.

YEW SPICE CUPBOARD

This very fine example dates from the reign of William and Mary and is one of the earliest known.

Such cabinets were made throughout the 18th century. By the 19th century, spices were also often kept in metal containers. Spice drawers are sometimes found in hutch racks.

The drawers have finely cut miniature dovetails — a mark of the cabinet's quality. The dovetail was a relatively new method of construction at the time it was made.

Oak Dough bin
Dough was placed in a dough bin in a warm part of the kitchen to rise before baking. This early 18th-century example is typical in shape, stands on turned legs, and is decorated with chip carving on each side. The lid, now separate, would originally have been hinged.

This cabinet is 19 inches (48 cm) high and would have stood on a table top or shelf.

Danish Pine Kitchen Table
This table is a classic shape which, combined with the use of doweled joints in its construction, suggests that it was made in the 1780s. But the original wooden handles point to a date of manufacture of about a century later.

The gilt handles are all original.

Dutch Ladderback Chair
Part of a set of six elm chairs, this piece is of a basic type found in both the old and new worlds. Although these chairs date from the 1840s, this style, with a rush seat, has been made since the late 17th century. Ladderback chairs were also made with solid seats.

The drawers of the built-in interior were used for storing exotic spices, which were always in solid form. They were a treasured commodity in the kitchen, hence the bolts and lock on the doors.

Miniature cabinets are often faithful reproductions of full-size pieces with all the details the same. Bun feet, frequently found on cupboards and cabinets, have been used here.

Irish Pine China Cupboard
The use of knot-free lumber, astragal glazing on the doors, and the molded cornice are all signs of quality, indicating that this is an above-average example of late Georgian pine furniture. The cupboard's blue-painted interior is traditional, and originally the exterior would also have been painted. The escutcheons are pewter.

SHAKER FURNITURE

Furniture made by the Shakers – a religious sect whose leader along with eight disciples left England in 1774 to go to North America – is still sought today. It can be found both in the aucton room, where it can command high prices, and in various stores that continue to sell Shaker products. Although the sect, which advocates celibacy, has all but died out, its cultural traditions survive.

Each Shaker community – by the 1820s there were 18, spread across eight of the United States – was self-sufficient, with its members making virtually everything they needed themselves. Furniture makers used local woods such as pine, maple, cherry, and walnut for their products. Everything they made was functional and practical, and largely free from the European influences that dominated much mainstream American furniture design. Each item was made solely for use, in the belief that appearance should be governed by function: there was no use of veneers or inlays, excessive turned decoration, or metal mounts. Furniture was finished either with light varnish or with a stained finish in colors such as red, green, blue, or yellow.

The reputation of Shaker furniture, which was largely founded on its practical and durable nature, spread outside the communities, and soon the Shakers were making chairs and other pieces for those they termed "World's People," or outsiders.

Shaker rooms were austerely efficient. Everything was stored away in chests and cupboards, and around each room was a peg rail on which chairs – deliberately made light but sturdy – were hung while the room was cleaned or when it was needed for a religious service; these pegs were also used to support hanging shelves and cupboards.

SHAKER MAPLE CUPBOARD WITH CHEST OF DRAWERS

Cupboards like this were often built into the rooms for which they were intended. Shakers put everything away when it was not being used.

The cupboard door is paneled.

Maple has been used here for the whole construction. It was commonly chosen for small, durable parts such as pegs and handles; pine was the popular choice for built-in items of furniture.

Some later Shaker furniture shows signs of the outside world's influence in slightly more elaborate turning or even fretwork.

The top is molded, but there is no extraneous decoration.

The cupboard has a single shelf inside. Clothes were hung from handmade hangers.

A central belief was that to make a thing well was in itself an act of prayer, so attention was paid to details.

The drawers are of varying size and depth. Clothing and other items were stored away by type and size so as not to waste any space.

This combination of cupboard and chest is fitted with a brushing slide.

SUGAR CHEST

The hinged top of this chest, made in Ohio in the late 19th century, has breadboard ends which allow the wood to shrink or expand along the grain according to the climate. The top part is divided into compartments, and the name implies that sugar   both white and brown – was stored in such chests, although sugar would have been affected by damp. Coffee was also sometimes kept in them. The cupboard and drawers below were also used for storage. Sugar chests are often fitted with locks – an unnecessary precaution in a Shaker community.

CHEST OF DRAWERS

Made in the early part of the 20th century – by which time declining numbers had forced some communities to advertise for new members, and physical comfort was being emphasized in addition to religious values – this pine and maple chest combines the simplicity of the Shaker way of life with a functional elegance. The moldings at both the top and bottom are applied.

SHAKER ROCKING CHAIR

Dating from the 1820s, this ladderback chair was made for a brother at the Hancock, Massachusetts, community. The dimensions of Shaker chairs often vary since each piece was "tailor-made" for the brother or sister who was to use it. The turned front posts end in mushroom finials which form integral parts of the posts; on later chairs, these were more usually applied. The chair is upholstered in the traditional manner with interwoven bands of cotton tape. The pommel finials on the back uprights were used for lifting the chair.

FRENCH PROVINCIAL FURNITURE

As a distinctive style, French provincial furniture emerged only in the early 18th century. Its forms and decoration are derived from the furniture made by Parisian craftsmen, either as a result of cabinetmakers seeing examples in a local noble's house or more often from one of the published books of designs. French provincial pieces are, however, always more sober than their Parisian counterparts.

Most provincial furniture is in the Louis XV style with cabriole legs and is made from various local woods such as walnut, chestnut, oak, beech, and cherry. The decoration is usually restrained, and many of the decorative motifs were used over a long period of time. Even when the more neoclassical Louis XVI style filtered down to the provinces, it had little effect on the way provincial furniture was made, other than to restrain the former exuberant curves a little. As a result, it is often difficult to distinguish between similar pieces of provincial furniture made in the 18th and 19th centuries.

In some of the larger provincial cities and towns, there were firms of *menuisiers* and *ébénistes* who made furniture in the Parisian style. Among the best-known of such makers are Pierre Nogaret of Lyons and the Hache family of Grenoble, whose work, although very fine, is not as sophisticated as that which inspired it.

MID 18TH-CENTURY MAHOGANY ARMOIRE

The arched molded cornice is centered by a carved basket of flowers. Carved decoration is a feature of pieces made in the second half of the 18th century, especially in northern France.

Armoires are large pieces of furniture: this one is about 8 feet 6 inches (2.5 m) high and 5 feet 6 inches (1.7 m) wide.

The woods used can help to identify the region in which provincial furniture was made. This example is mahogany, a wood not often used for such pieces. It suggests that this armoire was made near one of the major ports, in this case, probably Nantes.

Feet can vary from region to region and can be a useful guide to identifying where a piece was made. This armoire has scroll feet.

The shaped apron has carved acanthus decoration.

The molding of the paneled doors is in the rococo style. Molding is the most important decorative feature found on provincial furniture.

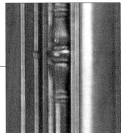

The use of brass or steel for hardware is a common decorative trait, and many armoires have brass hinges and ornate escutcheons similar to those here.

Provincial furniture is normally made from solid wood rather than from veneered carcasses.

Armoires were the most important piece of furniture in provincial homes; these traditional pieces can be traced back to the 14th century.

LOUIS XV FRUITWOOD TABLE

Provincial tables come in a variety of sizes, depending on the purpose for which they were made. With its rectangular plank top, waved frieze and cabriole legs, this example is typical of those used as side tables, although the presence of the slide on one of the sides suggests that it may have been used as a writing table.

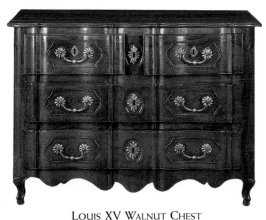

MID 18TH-CENTURY WALNUT BUFFET

Buffets are purely provincial pieces of furniture, not produced at all by Parisian or court *ébénistes*. This type, with paneled doors and molded top, is found in most regions, although there are local variations between them. Buffets with an upper cupboard or hutch section were also made.

LOUIS XV WALNUT CHEST

Unlike their more sophisticated counterparts, provincial chests usually have molded rather than marble tops. They also tend to be three drawers deep, although two-drawer-deep models were favored in Paris from the late 1720s onward. The decorative features – the molding, and brass handles and escutcheons – are common.

THE INFLUENCE OF THE ORIENT

In the 17th century, trade with the Orient by the Dutch East Indies Company, and others, resulted in the importation of Chinese and Japanese lacquer cabinets. These highly prized pieces were often placed on specially made giltwood stands. They were so greatly admired that European craftsmen made furniture with a "japanned" finish that imitated lacquer. The vogue for chinoiserie continued into the 18th century; in France in particular, panels of oriental lacquer were used to decorate case furniture.

The market for lacquer and oriental furniture was appreciated by the merchants trading with the Far East, who had Western-style furniture made in China for export back to Europe. In addition to such items as desks, coffers, and chairs, they also imported richly decorated lacquer screens. The tradition of importing oriental furniture has continued until the present day.

Japan, however, was closed to foreign travelers for two centuries, and the West first knew of its artistic traditions in the

EBONIZED DESK

The desk's top is inset with its original tooled leather. On many period desks, the leather has been replaced due to the wear and tear of regular use.

The smaller drawers are decorated with incised ribbing.

Furniture that was Western in shape, but with Japanese-inspired design motifs, was known as Anglo-Japanese. This desk is similar to the furniture in this style that Godwin designed for the firm of William Watt.

The legs are joined by fretted stretchers.

The drawer handles are electroplated and stylistically correct.

1850s through prints used to wrap china and from the goods on the Japanese stand at the International Exhibition of 1862. Artists working in the Aesthetic style were greatly influenced by Japanese simplicity and designed ebonized furniture which was rectilinear in shape and decorated with Japanese stylistic motifs.

The design of this desk, made in about 1875, is attributed to the architect E.W. Godwin, who by this time in his career had moved away from working in the Gothic style and was following the precepts of the Aesthetic movement.

The quality of the ribbing is only one indication that this table is well made, but the style was popular and much machine-made furniture of lesser quality can still be found.

The tapering circular legs stand on small brass castors.

CHINESE EXPORT BUREAU CABINET

The prototypes for this bureau bookcase, and others of similar design, came from Holland, Germany, and England, although the bombé-shaped lower section on this black, gold, and Nasiji lacquer example suggests that it was not originally made for the English market. Nasiji lacquer literally means pear skin; in this technique flakes of gold or silver are sunk to various depths in the lacquer (to lacquer each piece was a lengthy process and up to 30 coats could be applied). Most lacquer, as here, was applied to wood, usually one similar to pine which has a soft, even grain and can be smoothed easily. Sometimes lacquer was also used on pottery or metal, and objects were occasionally even carved from it. Export lacquer is usually not of such high quality as that made for domestic markets.

PAINTED EIGHT-LEAF SCREEN

Such large screens are commonly lacquered rather than painted. Here eight panels of mid-18th century Chinese wallpaper have been mounted to form a screen. Chinese wallpaper was imported in the 18th and early 19th centuries, and some rooms entirely decorated with it still exist. The paper has had extra decoration pasted on, and some of the insects are later additions. Screens have been, and remain, highly collectable.

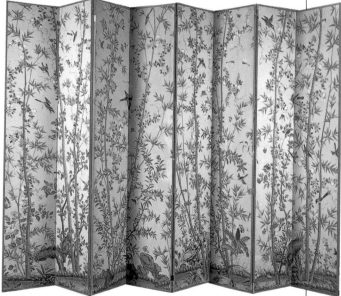

IMPERIAL PAINTING TABLE

This rare 18th-century table is made of jichimu, a hardwood with a feathered grain that has led it to be called chicken-wing wood. The intricate carving includes fretted scrolls, kui dragons, ruyi heads, and the Indian lotus. Western appreciation of traditional Chinese furniture has developed only since late in the 19th century.

UPMARKET PAINTED FURNITURE

Although the practice of painting furniture has a long history, it was not until the 18th century – influenced by the importation of lacquered pieces from the Far East – that painted furniture of the highest quality was made. In Italy, much furniture, particularly that produced by Venetian cabinetmakers, was decorated with a colored lacquered finish on a gesso ground on which flowers, pastoral scenes, or chinoiserie motifs were rendered in many different colors.

Many 18th-century Italian chairs and sofas have a painted finish, although in France gilding was preferred for decoration. Nevertheless, France led Europe in the quality of its painted furniture, particularly in that decorated with vernis martin. In this technique, evolved by the four Martin brothers, the color was stirred in with the varnishes or, if in powder form, mixed into a paste and then applied to the prepared surface. It could be used to decorate anything from a small box to a large room. Green was the most popular background color, and gold dust was sometimes added to imitate Japanese lacquer.

Vernis martin was copied in the 19th century, and many examples of furniture decorated with panels in the vernis martin manner can be found, although the quality is not as good as that of 18th-century pieces.

GEORGE III PAINTED SATINWOOD AND PARCEL-GILT SECRETAIRE BOOKCASE

The sides are not decorated, which indicates that this bookcase was intended to stand in a recessed alcove; most quality bookcases would also have appropriate decoration on their sides.

The hinged front drops to reveal a baize-lined writing surface.

Contemporary engravings of well-known houses were the inspiration for the paintings on copper panels.

This secretaire bookcase is in excellent condition and has had very little restoration. This is unusual, since paint becomes brittle, and cracking and signs of wear may appear with age on those parts that are used regularly. Many pieces of painted furniture have, as a result been, repainted or restored to enhance their appeal.

The central panel on the cupboard door depicts Cupid disarmed by Euphrosyne, and derives from an engraving of a painting by Angelica Kauffman. It, too, is on a copper panel.

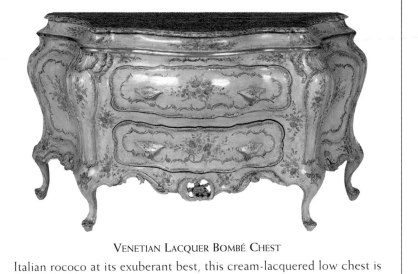

*Half-fan medallion painted
on the arched crest.*

*Acanthus leaf
cornice.*

*Attributed to the illustrator and
cabinetmaker George Brookshaw,
this is one of a pair of similar
secretaire bookcases made for
Piercefield Park, Monmouthshire,
Wales.*

*The Gothic glazing bars
are made of brass.*

*Ribbon-tied reeded edges on
the shelves are a pleasing
neoclassical device.*

*The floral panels reflect
Brookshaw's skill as a
botanical illustrator.*

*Turned feet are headed by
carved laurel collars.*

VENETIAN LACQUER BOMBÉ CHEST

Italian rococo at its exuberant best, this cream-lacquered low chest is decorated with scrolls and flowers in pastel hues – even the serpentine top is simulated marble. Italian furniture of this type did not have metal mounts or hardware but instead used paint to indicate such details. Despite its sophisticated outward appearance, such furniture is crudely made. It is still reproduced today.

PAINTED SATINWOOD PEMBROKE TABLE

At first glance, this appears to be an 18th-century table, but closer inspection reveals many anomalies that indicate it is probably from a later date. While in the 18th-century style, the painting is more stilted in execution than on a period piece, such as the secretaire bookcase on the left. And the fussy pattern and the medallions of ladies are a 19th-century conceit.

SIMULATED BAMBOO OPEN ARMCHAIR

This chair has the latticework sides and back associated with Chinese Chippendale (see the similarly shaped Chinese Chippendale chair on p. 23). But in fact the design is attributed to John Linnell, who made a set of 10 such chairs in 1767. The chair stands on turned legs and has turned stretchers. Simulated bamboo furniture enjoyed renewed popularity during the Regency period.

PAINTED COUNTRY FURNITURE

That painted furniture was not reserved for the rich is amply demonstrated by the painted country furniture of Austria, Bavaria, Switzerland, Scandinavia, and several other parts of Europe. In many areas, the tradition dates from at least the medieval era and continues to thrive to this day.

One decorative technique used on both town- and country-made furniture was graining, in which a simple wood was painted and then given a simulated grain with combs and brushes to resemble a more expensive one. But exuberant painting was also common. Much American furniture of the 18th and early 19th centuries was colored and decorated. Some pieces were copies of English styles; others were based on the European designs that were introduced by German immigrants, and are known today as Pennsylvania Dutch (a corruption of Deutsch).

In 18th-century Italy, the great love of painted furniture in upscale styles led to the development of a less expensive technique known as *lacca povera* (literally, poor lacquer), in which designs and motifs were cut out from prints and then colored before being glued to the carcass of a piece of furniture and varnished.

The enduring popularity of painted furniture, especially in country styles, has resulted in numerous pieces still being made in traditional styles.

CARVED PAINTED HADLEY CHEST

This rare piece was made as a hope or dower chest; such chests are known as Hadley chests after the Massachusetts town in which they were produced from about 1670 to 1740. This particular example dates from before 1710.

The molded top lifts to reveal a deep compartment for storage.

The sides of the case are paneled.

Stylized tulips and scrolls are used to decorate the two flanking panels.

Feet – here typical carved stile ones – are prone to wear.

The use of an oak case and pine parts is correct for this period of American furniture.

The carved overall decoration of leaves and flowers, in this case tulips, is a distinctive feature of Hadley chests.

Carved initials of the person for whom the chest was made usually adorn the central panel.

Chests of this type with a cofferlike top and drawers beneath are the predecessors of the chest of drawers.

The painted surface is probably original, although the central panel has a washed appearance. The use of red and black is typical for a chest of this date; brown and sometimes green were also used on these chests.

FEDERAL GRAINED POPLAR CUPBOARD

This grained cupboard was made in the 1820s in the mid-Atlantic states. The top cupboard doors open to reveal a mustard-painted interior The scalloped supports of the top section and the shaped apron and bracket feet give the cupboard an elegance that is derived from more sophisticated contemporary Federal furniture.

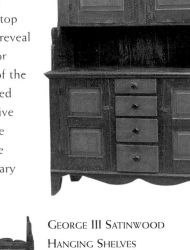

GEORGE III SATINWOOD HANGING SHELVES

These wall-mounted shelves were popular from the 18th century onward for the display of porcelain or books, and this provincial piece emulates more sophisticated examples. Although the use of satinwood indicates a certain quality – they were more usually made in mahogany – the naive painting indicates that this is not the work of a major cabinetmaker.

AUSTRIAN PAINTED HANGING CUPBOARD

Made in the Tyrol region of Austria in the first quarter of the 19th century, this carved and painted pine cupboard has traces of its original cream and dark green floral decoration. The arched top and waved apron are typical decorative features of these cupboards, which were made from the late 18th century onward.

AUSTRIAN PINE BIBLE BOX

Known as a Bible or deed box – although the term Bible box more strictly applies to one with a sloping top – this piece has its original wrought-iron hinges and a candlebox.

DISPLAY AND STORAGE

Toward the end of the 18th century, three pieces of occasional furniture evolved which could be used for similar purposes. The canterbury, used today as a magazine rack, was originally intended to hold music. The partitioned open top part held bound music while the apron drawer beneath could be used for loose sheet music. The whatnot or *étagère*, a tiered stand, was also originally used to hold either music or books and only in Victorian times came to be used as a stand for ornaments. The restrained early 19th-century style of canterburies and whatnots was replaced in Victorian times by the use of elaborate turning, pierced fretwork carving, and even marquetry panels.

The continued growth in the popularity of reading resulted in a demand for small bookcases that could be used in any room. Hence the development of standing, revolving bookcases which remained popular into the Edwardian era.

Trays have always been useful for carrying food, china, and glass from one room to another. The butler's tray is one of the most practical tray forms, with hinged sides and – usually – its own folding stand so that it can be used as additional serving space. Many early 19th-century trays have, in this century, been fitted with stands so that they can be used as coffee tables, thereby providing a practical solution to a 20th-century requirement for which there is no antique equivalent.

REGENCY ROSEWOOD FOUR-TIER WHATNOT

Some whatnots have adjustable tops that can be raised on a ratchet so that the whatnot can be used as a reading desk.

The four columns of this whatnot are ring-turned. Later 19th-century versions have more elaborate turning supporting the shelves.

Castors, here made of brass, mean whatnots can be moved around with ease.

*The supports end
in turned finials.*

*Victorian whatnots can be
wider than this example's
18 inches (47 cm) and less
deep than its 16 inches (40 cm).
Corner versions were also made.*

*Most early whatnots have
either three or four shelves, and
since some whatnots taper, the
shelves may be graduated.
Victorian whatnots sometimes
have backs with mirrors to
reflect the objects displayed
on them.*

*There is a drawer in the base
of this whatnot; some 19th-
century examples have
canterbury bases with
compartments and drawer.*

PAINTED REVOLVING BOOKSTAND

Based on a late 18th-century prototype, this
example in fact dates from the Sheraton revival of
a century or so later. The painted decoration is
obviously not as good as it would be on an 18th-
century piece and, at 5 feet (1.5 m) in height, the
bookstand is shorter than that which it copies.
This bookcase is interesting because it is made
from both West and East Indian satinwood – a
close-grained yellowish wood – at a time when
East Indian satinwood
alone was more
common.

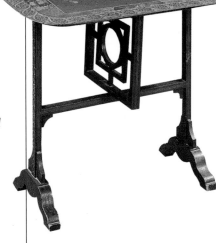

MID-19TH CENTURY PAPIER-MÂCHÉ TRAY

The surface of this red gilt tray is
decorated with a combination of leaves,
flowers, and pastoral scenes. It is a good
example of a popular 19th-century tray
type. Like many others, it has been
mounted on a later stand – here with a
pierced support and arched legs – for
use as a table.

QUEEN ANNE MAHOGANY
HANDKERCHIEF TABLE

This American table made around
the middle of the 18th century is a
variation of the gate-leg table. Its
triangular top means that it could stand
in a corner when not in use. When
opened with the triangular flap
supported by a gate-leg, it forms a
regular square-topped table.

REGENCY MAHOGANY CANTERBURY

The top of this canterbury is divided
into compartments by four dished,
slatted divisions, and it has a central
carrying handle. The ring-turned corner
columns are mirrored in the legs, which
end in castors. The apron drawer is a
common feature.

SMALL HOUSEHOLD FURNITURE

Sewing and embroidery were regular pastimes for well-to-do ladies in the 18th and 19th centuries, and the fruits of their labors can still be enjoyed today in such items as pictures and firescreens. In addition to a portable sewing box, most women also had a small sewing or work table. These tables, usually rectangular in shape, either had a box-shaped top with a hinged lid, or drawers with a work bag below in which they could keep work in progress. Many work tables had a sliding reversible top, so they could also be used as either game or writing tables, as well as a drawer in which sewing equipment could be stored.

Firescreens were an important feature of rooms and served the practical purpose of hiding fireplaces when they were not in use. Large sets of seat furniture were often made with an integral pair of firescreens, similarly upholstered. These large screens are often called cheval screens, from the French for horse, since they stood on four legs like a horse. Their frames are usually carved, and they often have needlework panels. A smaller type of firescreen that first appeared in the late 17th century was the pole screen, which had small panels that could be adjusted in height to protect the sitter from too much heat.

VICTORIAN PAPIER-MÂCHÉ WORK TABLE AND CABINET

A richly decorated cavetto-shaped compartment for storage is revealed when the top is opened.

Three drawers are concealed behind the doors. The bottom drawer contains built-in boxes which bear the maker's name MECHI, 4 LEADENHALL STREET. Mechi specialized in richly decorated small pieces of furniture.

Flowers, birds, and foliage adorn both the interior and exterior.

The cabinet stands on a barley-twist turned column which rises from the pedestal platform.

The whole top section can be lifted out to reveal a built-in interior with sewing implements.

Papier-mâché furniture, of which this is an excellent example, was highly popular in the 19th century. The black lacquered backgrounds can be painted or decorated with gilt or mother-of-pearl motifs.

Ornaments hang from the underside.

The elaborately painted top of the work table is dome shaped.

LOUIS XVI GILTWOOD FIRESCREEN
This cheval screen has a Beauvais tapestry panel worked from a design by Francesco Casanova, brother of the infamous Giacomo, who produced several sets of designs for the Beauvais Factory in the late 18th century. The arched top rail is centered by floral cresting with a pomegranate finial, a device repeated on the top of the side columns. These columns contain the counterweights which allow the screen to be raised.

The stand is decorated with painting and with gilt mounts.

REGENCY MAHOGANY WORK AND WRITING TABLE
This useful table, with a drop-flap top, elegantly combines two roles. It has a drawer which, when opened, can be used for writing, and the silk bag below indicates that it is also a work table. The veneers here are very well matched.

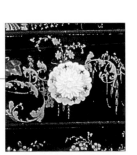

The drawer handles are shaped like flowers and made of gilt.

The four splayed legs end in scrolled feet and castors.

PARCEL-GILT WALNUT SIDE CHAIR
High-backed chairs such as this are often called *prie dieu* or prayer chairs, although they are not particularly practical for worship since there is no top ledge on the back to support either the user's arms or a prayer book, and at 4 feet (1.2 m), many are too high for comfort. They were often a showcase for the Berlin woolwork upholstery worked by their owner. Here parcel-gilding adds to the chair's value.

MARQUETRY INLAID SPOOL CAROUSEL
The octagonal base of this small – it is only 11 inches (28 cm) high – 19th-century canister is fitted with small drawers. Above are two open sections where spools of thread – here silk thread – can be stored neatly on ivory sticks.

DRINKING ACCESSORIES

Both alcoholic and non-alcoholic beverages were at least as important a part of daily life 200 years ago as they are now. Tea was a great luxury in the 18th century and therefore carefully husbanded. It was always dispensed with ceremony, the hostess adding tea to the boiling water from a special container or caddy.

These caddies, which were made in a variety of shapes and materials, were usually foil-lined to help keep the tea fresh (the exception was silver caddies, which were unlined). They were normally divided into two compartments, each with its own lid so that green and black teas could be kept separate.

During the 18th century, cabinetmakers introduced a range of stands and tables for use during the tea-drinking ritual, among which was a stand on which the caddy could be kept. Teapoys, which incorporated caddies, were introduced in the 19th century.

In the dining room where wine was consumed, furniture designed to keep and serve it was essential. Wine coolers for use during a meal were popular from the 1770s onward, as were cellarets which could be used both to store and to cool bottles. Cellarets are often oval or octagonal in shape, may be brass bound, and usually have a stand or legs. They have a lid which is either hinged or completely removable. In the early 19th century, the sarcophagus was a popular shape for wine coolers.

Another practical 18th-century piece of dining-room furniture was the mahogany bucket, usually brass-bound for strength, which was used to carry and store such diverse items as plates, peat, and wood.

WILLIAM IV CIRCULAR TEAPOY

The galleried top rises on an umbrella-type support. Many teapoys are rectangular, resembling the basic shape of a tea caddy. When closed, they can be mistaken for worktables.

The fitted interior contains two lidded compartments for teas and two glass bowls, one for sugar and one for blending the teas together.

Gadrooning decorates the b of the interior.

Most teapoys at this time were made of mahogany or rosewood.

Many 19th-century tea caddies were fitted with a glass bowl, but these are often missing.

This teapoy stands on a faceted column; most have baluster or pillar-shaped supports.

Carved scrolling feet are found here; some Victorian teapoys have scrolling legs.

The name teapoy derives from the Hindu word tepai, *meaning three-legged. The platform here is tripartite; quadruped platform bases are also found.*

Teapoys were first made at the end of the 18th century and continued to be produced throughout the Victorian era.

**REGENCY TORTOISESHELL
TEA CADDY**
The two compartments for
storing tea can be clearly seen
in this tortoiseshell caddy,
made in about 1815.
The bombé shape is
not common for
caddies. Generally,
19th-century tea
caddies are larger
than their 18th-
century counterparts.

**GEORGE III MAHOGANY
TRIPOD CADDY STAND**
This elegant stand combines
Gothic and Chinese motifs and
is supported by pierced scrolled
legs. The hinged top has a
flower-spray finial and a well
which holds a silver caddy;
although not original, it dates
from the 1770s, the same period
as the stand. The caddy is
attributed to William
and Aaron
Lestourgeon.

**GEORGE III SYCAMORE AND
CHECKER-STRUNG TEA CADDY**
This cube-shaped tea caddy is
inlaid with oval panels of burl
and harewood. There is a lidded
canister inside. Sometimes
caddies were made in the shape
of fruit, often carved from the
wood of the fruit tree
they represented.

**GEORGE III IVORY VENEERED
TEA CADDY**
This hexagonal-shaped tea
caddy is strung with horn. The
carrying handle and shield
inscription plate are both silver.

**GEORGE III SATINWOOD
TEA CADDY**
The simplicity of this tea
caddy with its canted corners is
relieved by the use of ebony
stringing and by the inlaid
sycamore and harewood panel
of flowers on the lid.

GEORGE III OVAL TEA CADDY
This satinwood caddy is inlaid
with floral marquetry on both
the lid and front. Tea was an
expensive item, so all caddies
were fitted with locks.

**GEORGE III MAHOGANY AND
BRASS-BOUND PLATE BUCKET**
Plate buckets can be distinguished
from other buckets – such as those
for peat – since they always have
an open section on one side so that
any plates stored inside can be
lifted out easily. Many plate
buckets were made by coopers
rather than furniture makers.

**IRISH MID-GEORGIAN
MAHOGANY BOTTLE STAND**
Used to carry up to eight
bottles, this tray has an
inverted lambrequin
border. The stand's shaped
frieze is carved with
foliate sprays and scrolls
on a punched ground. It stands on
cabriole legs ending in paw feet.

MIRRORS

Both decorative and practical, mirrors have fulfilled an important role since the second half of the 17th century. In the 17th and 18th centuries, frames were either inlaid with marquetry, or elaborately carved or gilded, with designs ranging from the grandeur of the baroque to the more fluid rococo carvings perhaps best encapsulated by Thomas Chippendale. In the 19th century, frames made from plaster on a wire base were common. Known as composition frames, they can be attractive, but are frequently damaged as the plaster chips quite easily.

French glassmakers used a system which allowed them to make fairly large plates of glass; until the 1770s when the French method was adopted in England and America. Mirrors made in those countries consisted of two or more small plates side by side. In the 18th century, glass was fairly thin, and the reflection obtained was darker than that given by the thicker glass plates that became common with 19th-century mirrors. The reflection is caused by lining the rolled glass with silver foil (mercury-coated tin foil).

Many period mirror styles are still reproduced today, including the early 19th century bull's-eye-shaped convex mirror, the gilded frame of which is often surmounted by an eagle; modern mirror glass, however, is much thinner than that which it tries to copy.

SOUTH GERMAN POLYCHROME MIRROR

The frame is a lively and well-executed example of baroque carving. Although the mirror's place of origin is not known for sure, it is thought likely it was made in southern Germany.

Damage on the mirror plate has been caused because the backing has worn off. There are two alternatives: either replace the mirror with a new plate or have the back re-silvered. Both affect the value of the piece, buit the latter is more esthetically pleasing.

The carved figures below the mirror plate represent Neptune, the Roman god of the sea, equivalent to the Greek Poseidon, and Amphitrite, the Greek sea goddess who was wife of Poseidon and mother of Triton. They are flanked by stylized roaring lions

GILTWOOD MIRROR
This 18th-century style of mirror was popular on both sides of the Atlantic. The mirror plate has a shallow beveled edge typical of 18th-century glass. The pounced ground of the frame is decorated with flower heads and foliage, and the broken-pediment cresting is centered with a Prince of Wales' feathers motif. The two candle sconces on the apron below the plate would have helped provide extra light when the candles were lit.

The crest and sides of the mirror frame are carved with entwined figures of eagles, mermen, and putti, in addition to dolphins, dragons, sea monsters, and even a seahorse.

SOUTH ITALIAN GILT-BRASS, CRYSTAL, AND CUT-GLASS MOUNTED MIRROR
This mirror with canted corners is a simpler Italian version of a 17th-century French design. Scallop shells and acanthus scrolls adorn the inner border, while the outer one features masks and pierced foliage. The space between them is decorated with fleurs-de-lis, flower heads, and starbursts.

The richly carved and pierced frame is decorated in polychrome; many such mirrors, however, are gilded.

FLEMISH GILTMETAL-MOUNTED EBONIZED MIRROR
The shape and style of this late 17th-century mirror have remained popular ever since. Mirrors such as this required the involvement of skilled workers both in wood and metal during their production. The decorative motifs include tulips.

A gilt slip around the mirror plate is common; slips are often decorated.

This mirror is large: it is 7 feet 6 inches (2.3 m) high and 5 feet 5 inches (1.65 m) wide.

BALTIC BIRCH, EBONIZED, AND PARCEL-GILT MIRROR
Made in the early 19th century, this mirror incorporates many neoclassical elements, including the *verre eglomisé* panel of putti. It would originally have rested on a table or mantelpiece, hence the paw feet.

OUTDOOR FURNITURE

Gardens have been furnished for centuries, with furniture generally falling into the same broad categories as that produced for interiors: some pieces are practical, others are purely ornamental.

Being able to sit, relax, and enjoy a garden has long been a priority. Stone or marble seats remain as popular today as they were 500 years ago. It is clear from contemporary paintings that in the 18th century wooden chairs and benches, both Windsor-chair types of rural origin and more sophisticated painted examples in the latest style, were taken outdoors. Wrought-iron benches were also used from the second half of the 18th century and became popular in the Regency period.

During the 18th century, garden design moved away from the formal elegance of Italian and French gardens toward the more natural-looking landscapes created by such English designers as Capability Brown, and furniture and statuary and other ornaments became less important. But by the mid-19th century, formal gardens were once again popular, which meant a renewed demand for these artefacts. The production of cast iron led to a proliferation of ornamental tables, vases, *jardinières*, and benches – a trend that continued throughout the 20th century.

CIRCULAR LEAD CISTERN

The presence of initials and a date are common features, but should not be taken at face value.

Lead was a popular material for garden ornaments in the early 18th century. Cisterns, however, may have been used indoors for storing drinking water.

Many cisterns have fitted with a faucet, but this has often been removed and the hole plugged so that the cistern can be used for other purposes.

Foliate motifs and swags are a common decorative feature.

Most early 18th-century lead cisterns are rectangular and made from four paneled sections. The lead is almost always thinner on reproduction pieces.

REGENCY REEDED WROUGHT-IRON BENCH
This elegant white-painted bench with a back of arches and ovals is typical of the seating found in the Romantic-style gardens of the early 19th century. The seat is slatted and the arm supports are elegantly shaped; like the back the arm supports reflect contemporary furniture designs.

ITALIAN WHITE MARBLE BENCH
Benches of this type have been made since the Renaissance. This example probably dates from the late 19th century, but such benches are still made today and are easy to age artificially. Other stones and artificial and ceramic materials, such as coade stone and terracotta were used for outdoor furniture in the 19th century.

GEORGE III STONE SUNDIAL
Sundials were a popular feature of 18th-century gardens in particular; they are much reproduced. The baluster-shaped column with circular spreading foot is topped by a bronze gnomon and a dial.

COALBROOKDALE CAST-IRON BENCH
This bench was made in England and is typical of much 19th-century cast-iron furniture by Coalbrookdale. Patterns vary from rustic leaf to an amalgam of revival styles, here Gothic. Cast-iron furniture was popular on both sides of the Atlantic and is reproduced today.

CONSERVATORY FURNITURE

There was enormous variation in the size of conservatories, which became a common feature of 19th-century homes; some were an integral part of the house. Many contemporary conservatories were furnished with wicker pieces that could also be used outside. Wicker furniture has been made since the earliest times, and production survived almost unbroken in rural areas, but its increased popularity in the 19th century meant that it was also made in towns.

The interest in far eastern artefacts, awoken by the Aesthetic movement, led to a range of bamboo furniture being made in the late 19th century, much of which was used in conservatories and gardens. While a loose cushion was used on many chairs to add to the sitter's comfort, chairs were also made with full buttoned upholstery.

Statuary, which has long been an important feature of formal gardens, also enjoyed a revival in the 19th century. Statues were not only dotted around the garden, they were also used to furnish conservatories and winter gardens. One example of the Edwardian fashion for indoor statuary is the fountain in the Palm Court of London's Ritz Hotel.

In addition to wood, wicker, bamboo, and cane, pottery, porcelain, and terracotta were also popular materials for seats and *jardinières*. These were made in a variety of styles and shapes, often reflecting the decorative trends of the day; others were copies, notably of the Chinese drum-shaped ceramic garden seats made during the Ming Dynasty (1368–1644).

MINTON MAJOLICA JARDINIÈRE

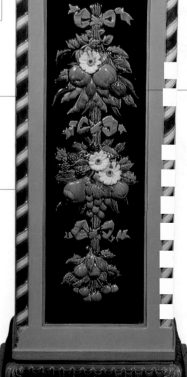

The neoclassical details, such as the rams' heads which are in fact the carrying handles, are in the 18th-century manner, but the overall concept with its heavy use of ornament is 19th century.

The base of the jardinière is modeled as four cherubs supporting the bowl on their shoulders.

Both pedestal and jardinière have survived together; this is often not the case — beware of marriages.

This example is in the Louis Revival style and was designed by Albert Carrier de Belleuse, a leading French sculptor who often made ceramic models for Minton.

The turquoise blue is one of the richest of the colored majolica glazes, developed at Minton from 1850 onward.

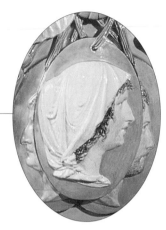

Molded relief decoration of overlapping oval medallions of rustic male and female heads adorn the bowl.

Made by Minton, this is an example of "majolica" for which the factory became famous in the second half of the 19th century.

There is a little damage to the piece, such as minor chipping and the toe of one of the four cherubs is missing, but this is acceptable. More serious damage would adversely affect value. Many pieces have been restored.

Molded panels of garlands of fruit suspended from bows decorate the square faces of the plinth and reflect the 19th-century enthusiasm for naturalism.

Stylized foliate decoration features on the base of the plinth.

MARBLE VENUS
This Italian white marble figure is classical in inspiration, but was probably made in the late 19th century. Marble statues are often chipped; this one has suffered damage to the wrist of its right hand, and the little finger is missing. Signs of weathering indicate that the figure was once part of a garden scheme, although it is quite easy to fake pitting and other signs of age in stone and marble pieces – many may not be as old as they appear.

VICTORIAN URN
The campana (bell) shape of this terracotta urn with its overhanging rim has been used in gardens since the mid-17th century. This is one of a pair stamped with the maker's mark LOCKHEAD BY CLAY COMPANY DUNFERMLINE. Traces of painted decoration remain, although this is unlikely to be original.

GERMAN BIRCH AND STAINED WOOD JARDINIÈRE
The term rustic is used to describe furniture that resembles wood. This example is typical of such pieces popular from the late 18th century onward. Here pine cones have been incorporated in the overall design.

LLOYD LOOM CHAIR
In 1917, the American Marshall Burns Lloyd patented a method of weaving together spun paper and wire to produce durable furniture for use in the house or outdoors. Known as Lloyd Loom, such furniture is still made, often to original designs. Most pieces are labeled, which can help buyers identify whether the piece is of early or more recent manufacture.

INDEX

ACKNOWLEDGMENTS

t top, b bottom, c center, a above, bl below, l left, r right

1–3 Christie's Images; 4 Nadia Mackenzie/National Trust Photographic Library; 5 Christie's Images; 6 l Phillips Auctioneers, r Christie's Images; 8 t, cla & cblr Clive Corless/Marshall Editions, cra, cbl & b Christie's Images; 9 t, tbl & ca Clive Corless/Marshall Editions, cbl, ba & b Christie's Images; 10 t & blt Christie's Images, ab & b Clive Corless/Marshall Editions, ca Phillips Auctioneers, cbl Christie's Images; 20–21 Christie's Images; 21 t Geffrye Museum, c & b Christie's Images; 22–27 Christie's Images; 28–29 Clive Corless/Marshall Editions; 30–31 Christie's Images; 31 t & b Christie's Images, 31 c Clive Corless/Marshall Editions; 32–33 Christie's Images; 33 tl Clive Corless/Marshall Editions; tr, bl & br Christie's Images; 36 t all Christie's Images, b all Bridgeman Art Library except bl l Fine Art Society/Bridgeman Art Library; 37 t all Christie's Images, b all Bridgeman Art Library except ac & ar Giraudon/Bridgeman Art Library; bl r "The Cortège of Orpheus" by Raoul Dufy © ADAGP, Paris and DACS, London 1996; 38–41 Christie's Images; 46–51 Christie's Images; 52–53 Christie's Images; 53 t & c Christie's Images, b Phillips Auctioneers; 54–55 Christie's Images; 56–57 Christie's Images; 57 t & b, Christie's Images, c Phillips Auctioneers; 58–59 Phillips Auctioneers; 59–63 Christie's Images; 68–71 Christie's Images; 70–71 Christie's Images; 71 t & b Christie's Images, br Phillips Auctioneers; 72–73 Christie's Images; 73t Phillips Auctioneers, c & b Christie's Images; 74–75 Christie's Images; 75 t Phillips Auctioneers, c & b Christie's Images; 80–85 Christie's Images; 85 t Phillips Auctioneers, c & b Christie's Images; 86–87 Christie's Images; 87 t & c Christie's Images, b Phillips Auctioneers; 88–89 Phillips Auctioneers; 89 all Christie's Images; 90–91 Christie's Images; 91 all Phillips Auctioneers; 96–97 Christie's Images; 97 t Mark Fiennes/National Trust Photographic Library, c & b Christie's Images; 98–99 Christie's Images, c Mike Caldwell/National Trust Photographic Library, b Christie's Images; 99 t Phillips Auctioneers; 100–103 Christie's Images; 104–5 Christie's Images; 105 tl & br Phillips Auctioneers, tr Christie's Images, bl Clive Corless/Marshall Editions; 110–111 Christie's Images; 111 t Phillips Auctioneers, c & b Christie's Images; 112–123 Christie's Images; 127 Clive Corless/Marshall Editions; 128–129 Clive Corless/Marshall Editions; 129 t Christie's Images, c & b Clive Corless/Marshall Editions; 130–131 Clive Corless/Marshall Editions; 131 t, ca & b Christie's Images, cbl Clive Corless/Marshall Editions; 132–133 Christie's Images; 133–135 Clive Corless/Marshall Editions; 136–137 Christie's Images; 137 t & c Christie's Images, b The American Museum in Britian; 138–141 Christie's Images; 142–143 Christie's Images; 143 t & c Christie's Images; 143 b Phillips Auctioneers; 144–145 Christie's Images; 145 tr & tl Christie's Images; 145 br & bl Clive Corless/Marshall Editions; 146–147 Phillips Auctioneers; 147 t Clive Corless/Marshall Editions, ca & b Phillips Auctioneers, cbl Christie's Images; 148–149 Phillips Auctioneers; 149 tl Phillips Auctioneers, tr Christie's Images, cra, crbl & b Clive Corless/Marshall Editions; 150 Clive Corless/Marshall Editions; 151 tr & br Christie's Images, tl Clive Corless/Marshall Editions, c & bl Phillips Auctioneers; 152–153 Christie's Images; 153 tl, tr & br Christie's Images, bl Phillips Auctioneers; 154–155 c Christie's Images; 155 b Neil Campbell–Sharp/National Trust Photographic Library; 156–157 cbl Christie's Images, 157 b Lloyd Loom of Spalding.

If the publishers have unwittingly infringed copyright in any illustration reproduced, they would pay an appropriate fee on being satisfied to the owner's title.